Brexit
Without
the Bullshit

Gavin Esler

First published by Canbury Press, 2019

Canbury Press,
Kingston upon Thames,
Surrey
www.canburypress.com

Cover: Rache Bowie/Canbury Press
Printed and bound in Great Britain
by Clays Ltd, Elcograf S.p.A.

ISBN: 978-1-912454-35-8 (Paperback)
978-1-912454-38-9 (Hardback)
978-1-912454-36-5 (Ebook)
978-1-912454-37-2 (Audiobook)

Brexit
Without
the Bullshit

Gavin Esler

CONTENTS

Introduction

INTRODUCTION

What is Brexit really going to look like? After 50 years of Britain arguing about Europe, what does leaving the European Union mean for you, me, our families, children, jobs, health care, and our daily lives? Shorn of the posturing and the promises, what are the profound changes that lie ahead? This book is not about the endless arguments over Brexit. It is about facts which will mould the future of our country. These facts, pleasant and unpleasant, should have been discussed properly when we held the referendum to leave in 2016. They weren't. For good or ill, they are vital now to understand the possible shape of a new United Kingdom. This, then, is not a book about the Brexit you may have thought you were voting for. It's about the Brexit we will get.

The most important tip I can give you is not to think of Brexit as an event. Brexit is a process. It will take years to unfold. It has already exposed serious weaknesses in our democracy and deep divisions within the British government, inside both the Conservative and Labour parties, between Scotland and England, in the communities of Northern Ireland, and between families, friends, work colleagues and neighbours. These wounds will take time to heal. Formally leaving the

EU is the beginning – not the end – of creating a new story for the UK, making new trade, security and other arrangements with Europe, with the rest of the world, and with each other.

We need to think about making the most of the opportunities ahead. But we also need to consider the realities of ending a relationship which has lasted almost half a century. The Brexit negotiations have raised legitimate fears that we may lack skilled trade negotiators and politicians who are up to the job. Questions have been raised about whether the competence and standing of the United Kingdom has been so diminished that future trade relationships with such powers as the US, Japan and China may reveal further weaknesses on our part. Hearings by the American negotiator, the US Trade Representative, have revealed American businesses see great opportunities in Brexit – for them. Well-funded American interest groups representing agri-business, pharmaceuticals, health care and high-tech industries have been lobbying the US government. They are openly demanding the UK accept American food standards and reject European ones as the price of a future trade deal. A key demand is for American firms to be able to carve out chunks of the National Health Service.

Making the best of Brexit, then, is clearly not as easy as some of the more inventive 'have our cake and eat it' promises and 'take back control' slogans. But we need to give it our best shot. That means ignoring the slogans and focusing on a sober assessment of the challenges ahead.

Who and What We Are Up Against

Brexit requires the biggest transformation of the UK since World War Two, something far more ambitious than Margaret Thatcher's 1980s shock therapy, when she sold off council housing, privatised state industries, checked union power, liberated the Falklands, and confronted the Soviet Union. Brexit has already involved rethinking the United Kingdom's foreign, economic, trade, migration, health and social care policies and security relationships. It also means turning thousands of European Union laws and regulations into workable British equivalents.

During the 2016 Brexit campaign, the Conservative Cabinet minister Michael Gove claimed that the British people 'have had enough of experts.'[1] Yet in the ensuing years, experts have been exactly what we have needed, and often sorely missed. In trade matters, the absence of expertise has been exposed. 'Rolling over' existing EU trade deals with Japan and Turkey to apply to the UK after Brexit has proved impossible for British trade negotiators. To make Brexit work now, Britain needs to secure a degree of positive cooperation from the remaining 27 EU members. Given the acrimony and derision which British government efforts have directed at EU leaders, this will not be easy.

Since the Brexit vote I have travelled widely across Europe, to Belgium, Estonia, France, Germany, Holland, Ireland, Italy, Norway, Spain and Sweden. British people sometimes forget that politicians and many ordinary citizens in these countries read our newspapers, watch BBC news, and often have very positive views about British culture and competence. Our reputation for practical hard-headedness has taken a knock. Comedy programmes have poked fun at our position and the eccentricities of our parliament. Irish children's TV has explained Brexit in terms understandable to five-year-olds. French, Dutch and Swedish cartoonists caricature leading Brexiters as cliches of a stuck-in-the-past Britain. Sober German news magazines have taken to describing the leading Brexit advocate Jacob Rees-Mogg as 'das lebendes Fossil,' the living fossil.

Beyond the jokes and insults, the serious point is that making Brexit work is daunting. The central difficulty is not principally because the other heads of government in the European Council, the Merkels, Macrons and Varadkars, or EU negotiators like Michel Barnier and Sabine Weyand want to punish Britain. Brexit is difficult because all these prime ministers and parliaments in the 27 other member states have their own political pressures and priorities. The post-Brexit future of the UK is not top of anyone's list, except our own. We must understand that and proceed in a spirit of constructive competence with our EU neighbours, not resentment or suspicion.

We will need to be industrious. Brexit will touch our homes and kitchens, our restaurants and supermarkets, our hospitals, schools, and workplaces. An estimated 12,000 EU regulations which have been operating in the UK for years will have to be copied into UK law. Every one will have to be re-evaluated, possibly re-drafted or scrapped. And any legal gaps or errors could cause unforeseen problems, leading to costly lawsuits tying up our courts and legal experts for years to come.

Brexit, therefore, requires detailed decisions on everything from regulations about food and the pricing and availability of medicines to how we boost jobs by selling goods and services abroad, border security, holiday travel, the validity of qualifications, licences and insurance policies. Potentially, it complicates even the most sensitive private matters including marriage, divorce and child custody cases for Britons in relationships with EU nationals.

Brexit affects not just the 66 million UK citizens, but an estimated 3.8 million EU nationals living here, too. Some EU citizens have already left, fearing they are less welcome or that Britain will make itself poorer and less attractive. A builder in London told me that none of his six contractors who went home to Poland at Christmas 2018 came back to Britain. They told him that the drop in the value of the pound after the referendum in 2016 meant the UK was no longer such a lucrative place to work. (The pound slid 18% from $1.50 in June 2016 to $1.27 in May 2019.)

What £1 buys

$1.50 — 2016

$1.27 — 2019

Moreover, Brexit has not only changed forever our future relationship with the other 27 nations and the nearly 450 million people who remain in the EU. It has also changed relationships among the peoples of the British Isles, which could well alter the way we live and work for generations. The United Kingdom is divided. England and Wales voted to Leave. Northern Ireland and Scotland voted to Remain.

In Northern Ireland, nationalists such as Sinn Fein are agitating for another vote on whether to join the Irish Republic, re-opening a painful wound in British politics.

In Scotland, nationalists are demanding another referendum on independence, arguing that Brexit represents a 'material change' since Scots voted to stay in the UK in 2014. The Scottish National Party may not be able to dissolve a political union between Scotland and England dating back to the Union of Parliaments of 1707. But the possibility creates further uncertainty. It opens up the prospect of an EU border between England and Scotland, with an independent Scotland determined to eject Britain's nuclear deterrent from its base near Glasgow.

A Very Un-British Beginning

One of the reasons Brexit is so divisive is that we confirmed our entry into what was then the European Economic Community (EEC) or 'Common Market' through the very un-British mechanism of a referendum in 1975. With a degree of political symmetry we are leaving it in the same way. For centuries, Britain was governed without national referendums – as a representative democracy. We elect MPs to make decisions on our behalf. If we dislike these representatives we vote in a new government. In 1973, the UK joined the EEC after a decision taken by Edward Heath's Conservative government. But such were the political divisions then, and the fault lines in both Conservative and Labour parties, that when two years later Labour came to power under Harold Wilson, he launched what was considered a unique constitutional experiment. The result of the UK's first ever national referendum was overwhelming. Two thirds of British voters chose to remain in the EEC.

That clear verdict was overturned in the Brexit referendum of 2016 by a much narrower majority, by 52%, 17.4 million voters, for 'Leave' against 48%, 16.1 million voters, for 'Remain'. The question on the ballot paper appeared clear enough:

'Should the United Kingdom remain a member of the European Union or leave the European Union?'

The result endorsed the principle of leaving, but gave no clue to what that would mean in practice. The people who voted Leave were clear in their own minds at least what they were voting against. The EU has never been popular in Britain. But it is impossible to believe that all 17.4 million Leavers agreed precisely on what they were voting for, since it took Theresa May two years in Downing Street to come up with her own Brexit policy, which pleased almost no-one.

Since 2016 I have travelled extensively within the UK, from Cornwall to Aberdeen, taking in Glasgow, York, Leeds, London, Wales and Northern Ireland and many places in between. I have been to 'Brexit Central', Kent and parts of the Midlands and 'Remain Central', Edinburgh and north London. In many conversations with Leave and Remain voters it is striking that there are still multiple versions of what we think or fear Brexit might mean. Millions of British people want the chance to vote again. Six million signed an online petition to Revoke Article 50 and end the process. Many I have chatted to feel disconnected from politics and politicians, especially the traditional political parties. As a carpenter put it to me:

'They never listen and Brexit was my chance to be heard.'

He enthusiastically voted Leave, despite not usually voting in general elections. The Leave campaign slogan 'Take back control' struck a chord with him and millions of others while the inept Remain campaign was based largely on doom-laden projections about our future, branded 'Project Fear' by opponents who accused it of scaremongering. Neither side truly confronted the reality of what leaving the EU would mean. This book is an attempt to do just that. It is a guide for those of us who need to move from principles to practicalities. Some of it involves a degree of informed guesswork. Even after almost three years of discussions much remains to be settled, and there may be many twists and turns ahead in the Brexit road. But these are the best available facts now, laid out to help us all understand what is going on and what awaits us.

• *Any errors or omissions please contact me at gavin@gavinesler.com*

1. BREXIT & OUR FOOD

Early on a Saturday morning at a market in Deal, a small seaside town in Kent, traders are setting up stalls. The air is filled with the smell of fresh rolls and sizzling sausages made by a local butcher. The lamb and beef is all local. The Swedish woman who sells cardamom and cinnamon buns is also now a local, a town resident. So, too, is the Frenchman who sells wine. On the corner of the market, the fruit stall has 'Kent Apples,' 'Leeks Picked in Deal,' and other local produce. It's a garden of England scene, similar to many weekend markets across the UK, but with one striking difference. From the town beach on a clear day you can see the white cliffs of Cap Blanc Nez and Cap Gris Nez in France, less than 30 miles away. In between is one of the world's busiest sea routes, the English Channel.

Deal's Saturday markets and historic castle attract day-trippers from London – just over an hour away on the high-speed train – and also cars and coaches from France, Belgium, and elsewhere in mainland Europe. Ferries from Calais to Dover take less than 2 hours and outside peak times the crossing can be cheap – £50 return for a family of four in a car. Local Kent residents and some from London make the day-trip in the opposite direction, taking the ferry to France for lunch, then load the car with wine and cheese, and return in the early evening. Another trader, an Englishman, sells clothing and shoes sourced on French trips. So does one of the shops on the main street. There is a stall selling French and English cheeses.

People on the Kent coast have been doing this kind of trading – and also plenty of smuggling – in and out of France and the Low Countries for centuries. Notoriously, they even did so when England and France were at war. The exploits of smugglers and pirates are celebrated by signs throughout the town and at castles at Deal and Walmer, built by Henry VIII to repel cross-Channel invaders. Today, a Border Force cutter sits offshore looking for illegal migrants who risk crossing the busy shipping lanes for what they hope will be a better life in England.

Whatever politicians, privateers and warriors were up to in past centuries, English coastal dwellers did not seek or require permission from any government to exploit their closeness to France. Nor did they need membership of the European Union. After Brexit, cross-Channel trade here will continue, and life will go on – but Brexit does change important aspects of how we trade with Europe. Those changes affect everything and everyone in Deal's Saturday morning market, and in markets and supermarkets and homes and offices up and down the country, including how we source the food we eat, the health regulations governing its transportation, the tariffs that may be put on it, the identity of the people who do the farming, harvesting, buying and selling, and of course the price.

Freedom of Movement

Even before Brexit occurs, as part of the preparations, the French wine seller and the Swedish bun maker fell into the category of those who needed to apply for the right to stay in the UK. EU citizens previously already enjoyed this right under Europe's single market. It enshrined 'four freedoms' – the free movement of goods, services, capital and workers. The first of these, freedom of movement, is why our French wine importer or the stall-holder who brings in French clothing can make a living at a street market in England with a minimum of bureaucracy and form-filling. And why any of us can go on a quick 'booze cruise' to France, retire to the Costa del Sol, or find work in Germany, as unemployed tradesmen did in *Auf Wiedersehn, Pet*.

Broadly, most British people had few complaints about the first three of these freedoms, but pro-Brexit politicians and sections of the conservative press were less enthusiastic about the circulation of people than trade. Freedom of movement became particularly contentious after 10 countries joined the EU in 2004, eight of which were from eastern Europe (Czech Republic, Estonia, Hungary, Latvia, Lithuania, Poland, Slovakia and Slovenia). Hundreds of thousands of their citizens headed to the UK to work for higher wages. Young workers from Poland or Romania ended up picking vegetables and berries for the stall holders at the Kentish markets.

The British government says that although freedom of movement will end with Brexit it has no intention of deporting EU nationals currently in the UK. Similarly, EU governments say they respect the rights of UK citizens in their countries. But the relationship and the status of British people in Europe and that of EU citizens here in Britain has already changed (see EU Settlement Scheme in next section). Travel to the Continent will too. In the past, Britons and other EU citizens could travel without passport checks across the Schengen Area, which covers most of the EU and some non-members such as Norway and Switzerland, but not the UK. A British driver who took their car on the ferry to France could visit Berlin or the Russian border with just a driving licence.

Almost all of the countries on the way, such as France and Germany, accept euros. Again, Britain opted out of the euro. Britain's position in Europe – with opt outs on border control and the common currency – was considered by many to be fortunate. Jakob von Weizsäcker, chief economist at Germany's finance ministry, quipped:

> 'The irony [of Brexit] is that the two most disappointing areas of the EU – the common currency and Schengen – were the two areas from which Britain had most insulated itself.'[2]

Rule Changes: The Settlement Scheme

In preparation for Brexit, Britain changed the rules for the vast majority of EU citizens resident in the UK. Some 350,000 from the Irish Republic were exempted because of the historical closeness of Ireland and Britain. However the remaining 3.5 million EU nationals were asked to apply to an EU Settlement Scheme to continue living in the UK after 30 June 2021. If their application was successful, they would receive either 'settled or pre-settled status.'

A £65 fee to register caused great irritation to some. A Labour peer, Lord Wood of Anfield, complained that he was expected to explain to his octogenarian German-born mother, who had happily moved here after marrying an Englishman, that she would have to pay £65 to continue living where she had done for decades. After a public outcry in 2018 the Settlement Scheme fee was dropped[3]. But that means instead of being self-financing by pulling in an estimated £225 million in fees, it's become a costly and (to applicants) an unwelcome Brexit burden which affects around 6% of people currently living in the UK. Each of them must now fill in new forms to legitimise their existence. A Romanian care worker told me that she was at first very alarmed at the registration process, then offended but finally – since Britain has been her home for many years – she completed the paperwork and has been told she can remain.

What Has This To Do With Food?

The new rules affect many of the people who pick the plums, apples, pears, tomatoes, berries and other produce on sale at our local food markets and in supermarkets. Residents from the other 27 EU states play a very significant (though often unseen) role in food production. In fact, 41% of workers in food and drink processing come from the EU27.[4] When it comes to the least glamorous, sometimes backbreaking jobs they are almost two thirds (63%)[5] of the workforce for members of the British Meat Processors Association, and almost all those working for members of the British Summer Fruits Association.[6] Vets are especially likely to be from the EU27.

Veterinary Checks on Meat

An estimated 95% of the vets certifying animals fit for slaughter in the UK are non-British EU nationals. These are the people who check that animals are healthy enough to be eaten by British carnivores or exported to the European mainland where British beef and lamb are in demand. That means that the health and animal welfare standards of UK lamb, beef, poultry and pork depend on a group of highly trained people who have voluntarily come here and who have now been told they must jump through a bureaucratic hoop in order to stay.

More worryingly, perhaps, depending on the nature of the deal struck (or not struck) with Brussels, Brexit could dramatically increase demand for veterinary inspections of meat. Nigel Gibbens, formerly the Chief Veterinary Officer, estimated that the volume of products requiring veterinary export health certification could increase by up to 325% after Brexit. Even with a satisfactory final deal, in future there will be a far heavier paperwork load – because 'a UK exporter of an animal product to the EU will need to have an Export Health Certificate alongside the consignment.'

That additional workload comes on top of an existing vet shortage. In 2018, the Major Employers Group, which represents big vet practices and corporate groups, found its members had vacancies for 11.5% of vets and 7.6% of veterinary nurses.[7] Overall, it estimates that about a third of its members' workforce is non-UK EU graduates.[8] What's more, it says that EU trained vets are more likely than British colleagues to work full time, meaning their overall contribution is even higher than the figures suggest. EU nationals are almost a quarter, 22%, of those working as veterinary academics, teaching the British vets of tomorrow.[9]

The British Veterinary Association (BVA) is monitoring further shortages and has asked for government action to ensure EU vets can continue to be recruited. It points out that vets are important to the economy: livestock and the horse industry alone generate £21 billion per year.

Britain will hope to continue to attract vets from the EU and elsewhere. But the concerns in the profession and in the meat industry are real, and as those of us who own pets know already, insurance costs and vet bills for our animals can be crippling. If you own a dog, horse, cat or other pets, you may also find Brexit brings a shortage of the qualified people who are trained to treat your much loved animal. We deal with pet passports in *Chapter 6: Brexit & Travel*.

When more than 1,200 British vets were polled in 2018, 96% said the best option for Britain would be to remain in the EU. As *Farmers Weekly* put it:

'The veterinary profession is particularly challenged by Brexit, given that half of new vets registered by the Royal College of Veterinary Surgeons each year are EU nationals, as are 95% of vets working in abattoirs.' [10]

Fruit and Veg

EU citizens are just 6% of the population but make up about 8.5% of the total UK workforce across all industries.[11] That's because French, Germans, Spanish, Polish and other EU citizens who live here are more likely to be employed or self-employed than native-born British citizens. They are younger and have more skills, according to the Migration Advisory Committee, an independent public body which advises the UK government. EU migrants often do some of the low-paid and low-status jobs British workers prefer to avoid, such as cleaning and care-home work. According to the National Farmers Union, only 1% of those picking fruit and vegetables in season are UK nationals.

By providing cheap, willing labour, workers from other EU states have expanded our economy. For many years British production of labour-intensive crops such as asparagus, cherries, raspberries and strawberries fell. But production started rising again when the new, mostly eastern European countries joined the EU in 2004. New cheap labour from the Continent has powered a boom in home-grown production of some of our favourite fruit and veg.

Many of the more recent arrivals among farm workers have come from poor EU countries, especially Bulgaria and Romania. The nationality of migrant workers tends to vary over time. Where my parents lived in a small town in Norfolk, most of the seasonal agricultural harvest workers were Portuguese. Some stayed permanently and set up a Portuguese cafe and shop. But after 2004 most of the Portuguese left the fields and food processing factories and were replaced by Lithuanians. The Lithuanians were said to be cheaper, but they proved just as entrepreneurial as the Portuguese. Within months a Lithuanian cafe and deli replaced the old Portuguese establishment.

A majority of British farmers voted for Brexit in 2016, but many have become increasingly concerned about who will pick their fruit and vegetables. In the final quarter of 2018, the number of EU nationals working in the UK fell by around 61,000 year-on-year[12]. There was a steep fall in employees from the eight eastern European countries that joined the EU in 2004. They numbered 869,000, compared with a record high of 1.05 million in July-September 2016, just after the referendum. Jonathan Portes, professor of economics at King's College London, said the overall data confirmed a 'significant 'Brexit effect' on migration from the EU' to the UK. 'Brexit-related uncertainty and insecurity,' he said, had made the UK a 'less attractive place for EU citizens to live and work.' What some newspapers have referred to as the 'Brexodus' of EU citizens has hit food production particularly hard. By 2017 there was a shortfall of 12.5% of seasonal workers and farmers reported some produce was left to rot in fields.[13]

The UK has low levels of unemployment and, as farmers will readily tell you, many Britons simply do not like to toil in the fields on jobs with limited prospects and low wages. To address these shortages, the government began a pilot scheme in 2019-2020 to issue visas of up to 6 months for 2,500 non EU/EEA citizens. That is a fraction of the 60,000 field workers required by British farmers[14].

One appeal of supposedly 'Global Britain' after Brexit is that any shortfall in, say, Romanian or Lithuanian strawberry pickers could (if demanded by landowners and permitted by the government) be met by an influx of workers from other countries – perhaps Turkish or North African labourers, or fruit pickers from the Caribbean and Pakistan. On the fertile plains of Lincolnshire, which saw a large influx of EU27 agricultural workers, voters enthusiastically backed Brexit in 2016; in the market town of Boston 75% voted Leave[15]. But those voters who wanted Brexit to end or significantly reduce immigration, especially low-skilled immigration, may be disappointed if Lithuanian or Romanian migrants are simply replaced by counterparts from north Africa or Asia.

And if the EU workers are not replaced, farmers will have to change some of the crops they plant. In recent years, if you ate British meat or berries (the local produce we often cherish), then the food on your plate had almost certainly arrived thanks in some way to European workers, from fruit pickers to vets to meat processors or those in frozen food factories. The optimistic case for Brexit and food is that most of the skilled EU vets will choose to stay in our abattoirs making sure our beef, lamb and pork is good to eat, and in some way the existing shortage of vets will be addressed. And if British farmers pay enough, presumably they will find someone to do the low-paid seasonal work currently done by Romanian and Bulgarian harvesters. But hard-pressed farmers have repeatedly warned that they may have to raise wages, which inevitably will be passed on to British shoppers in the form of higher prices.

Farmers also worry that after Brexit the EU may put up tariffs or other barriers on British food exports. But assuming that over the next few years when Brexit begins to take effect we are capable of sorting out all the new paperwork, and find the right workers, how much will our food actually cost? The answer, given all these factors and the slide in the value of the pound, is that it is likely to be more expensive.

What Will Our Food Cost?

Half the food we eat in Britain is produced in the UK, and half comes from all other countries. Some crops – coffee, ginger, bananas, olives – obviously do not thrive in our climate. Other which do thrive – tomatoes, berries – are seasonal. Back in 1973 when we first joined the Common Market most British shoppers did not expect to eat strawberries or tomatoes all year round, but many of us do now. When UK produce is out of season, 90% of lettuces, 80% of tomatoes and 70% of soft fruit is sourced from, or via, the EU. British supermarkets stock vast numbers of Spanish tomatoes and Dutch hothouse cucumbers. Across the year, almost a third of the food we eat comes from the EU (30%). On the Kent market stalls in among the local beetroot, Kentish cob nuts and potatoes are imported Italian lemons, Spanish oranges, Greek olive oil, French cheeses and wines, and spices from Asia and elsewhere.

Following Brexit, tariff changes or bottlenecks at the Channel ports could badly disrupt these food supplies from Europe. If this disruption happens or prices rise, we could theoretically import more food from outside Europe. Such supplies are currently quite small. A mere 4% of British food comes from Africa, 4% from North America, 4% from Asia and just 1% from Australia[16]. For these far away continents to make up shortfalls in EU food would demand such drastic changes to our food import policies and inspection regimes. Transport costs would also be higher. To put it simply, we are unlikely to be eating large amounts of Australian or American tomatoes any time soon.

Brexit may, however, change the way we think about food. Meurig Raymond, president of the National Farmers Union, points out that because the UK is a densely populated country: 'We will never be self-sufficient in food production… Can we increase self-sufficiency? Definitely.'[17] Others, such as Professor Tim Lang of City University, believe self-sufficiency is technically possible – but would demand such profound changes to our eating habits, like eating meat only once a week, that it is currently unthinkable. (A national switch towards vegetarianism was not a notable selling point of Brexit.)

Both Meurig Raymond and Professor Lang suspect that in the immediate post-Brexit period the price of British food will rise. Professor Lang believed that could lead to a rethink of eating habits:

'When food prices rise and European food markets desta-
bilise as a result of Brexit, I think more people will begin to
take food issues more seriously.'[18]

Some would welcome such a rethink, but, again, the
destabilisation of food supplies was not advanced as a
reason to vote to leave the EU.

On the Kent market stalls food prices have already
gone up because sterling has dropped. There is anecdotal evidence that this fall in the pound's value has en-
couraged some EU farm workers to leave Britain and
seek work elsewhere, since their pay, if sent back home
in euros, has also fallen. Transport costs have also risen
as a result of an increase in fuel prices denominated in
US dollars, though the oil price is volatile.

But the real sticking point about future food supplies
appears to be increased checks, bureaucracy and border controls creating delays, increased food wastage and
occasional disruption of supply. The UK government's
own advice gives a sense of the problem it foresees.

What is the Government Doing About This?
The UK government has warned British importers and
exporters that life is about to become more bureaucratic, at least in the short term. In February 2019, it urged
businesses to get a UK Economic Operator Registration and Identifications number 'so you can continue
to import or export goods.' It warned that those importing animals and animal products would no longer
be able to use the EU's Trade Control and Export Sys-

tem to notify the UK authorities of an import. Consignments of live animals, meat, fish, or shellfish would need to be checked at Border Inspection Posts. Some goods would need to enter the UK via Designated Points of Entry. Others would not.

When it comes to exports, the new systems for exporting animals, meat, and fish proposed by the UK government are eye-wateringly complicated and I will not detail them here. But what shines through is that Britain has begun to take the possibility of disruption to our food supplies seriously. The rest of the EU is less concerned for obvious reasons, and this in itself could cause problems for importers and exporters. For example, British food exporters have been told that consignments in future will need to enter the EU via a Border Inspection Post. The trouble is that the most popular EU port for British goods, Calais, just 26 miles from Dover, is not currently an accredited Border Inspection Post. Whether French officials re-designate Calais as a BIP with a sense of urgency remains to be seen. While in the single market, that kind of bureaucracy would never have been a problem.

Food Banks and Food Poverty

Food inflation hit a five-year high of 2.5% in 2019, partly as a result of bad weather. For many reasonably well-off British people the impact of such rises is negligible – a few pounds on the weekly grocery bill. But for millions of less affluent British people food prices are crucial and in the winter can set up a galling choice of heating or eating.

My children's school asks for 'shoe box' collections of food and toiletries, a few items packed into old shoe boxes. Jack Monroe, who calls herself the 'Bootstrap Cook,' has dedicated the profits of her latest book of recipes made from tinned goods to food banks. The Trussell Trust operates more than 400 food banks in the UK and says the number of users went up from tens of thousands in 2010 to half a million by 2017. The total number of UK food banks is not clear – some are ad hoc affairs, but estimates suggest it may be around 2,000[19].

The British government does not routinely collect data on food poverty, but according to food charities and research by international agencies 10% of children in the UK are living with severe food insecurity. This is more than double the average for other EU countries, which is just 4%. In 2017, Unicef, a United Nations body, claimed that the UK was facing a rising tide of malnutrition that damaged children's lives. Changes to social security, especially the introduction of universal credit, are blamed for exacerbating food poverty.

The correlation between these worsening statistics on food poverty and Brexit has been challenged by Brexit's supporters. If Brexit does lead to higher food prices, though, it is hard to see how it will lead to anything other than the existence of more hungry families and more hungry children unable to concentrate at school.

Dig For Victory

There remains the optimistic case of Brexit inspiring some kind of new agricultural revolution in which British farming and eating habits change.

We currently import almost 10 times more fruit and vegetables than we export. In 2016, imports were £10.3 billion while exports totalled just £1.1 billion – a gap of £9.2 billion[20]. Leaving the single market without agreeing a trade deal with the EU after the transition period would probably push up the cost of these imports. Some Brexit advocates claim that we would be happy as a nation to do without foreign-produced cucumbers, tomatoes and lettuce. This seems doubtful, and even if true, only a small part of the picture.

Fresh strawberries, raspberries, and blackberries make up the major fruit group imported to the UK from the European Union. Spain supplied 37.5% of berry imports, 40% of the trade in citrus fruit, and more than 50% of apricots, cherries and peaches. France sends the UK about a quarter of our apples and pears, and Spain and the Netherlands produce more than half of the onions, garlic and leeks. The Netherlands produces a large amount of our cucumbers and carrots[21]. The UK imports more food than it produces in every food group, including meat, cereals, fish, coffee, tea, cocoa, dairy and eggs – except beverages. Exports of beverages are extremely high thanks to the worldwide demand for Scotch whisky.

As we noted, farmers groups in Britain have for years worried about the slow decline in the amount of food we produce domestically. In the long run Brexit may help to reverse this trend, but in the short to medium term imports will be required to fill the seasonal gaps of Britain's favourite foods. Producers in Spain and the Netherlands will still want to sell us food – but there is no certainty about price.

Once we leave the single market a new trade deal will need to be negotiated with the EU in order to avoid tariffs. Such a trade deal will presumably include UK food exports, our excellent beef, salmon, fish, whisky and the other sought after food we do produce. Imports from the US, Australia and New Zealand or African countries could rise and fill some of the gaps, and British farmers will undoubtedly want to rise to the challenge, especially since so many voted for Brexit.

The Common Agricultural Policy and the Single Market

One reason British farmers voted for Brexit is that leaving the EU means no longer being bound by the rules of the Common Agricultural Policy. For many Brexit advocates the CAP is the EU's original sin. It takes EU taxpayers' money and gives it to farmers, sometimes to grow things, and sometimes to help the environment. Historically, the CAP has often seemed unfair and skewed towards big farmers and their bigger lobbying groups, especially in France.

The UK Government has guaranteed to match CAP funding for British farmers in 2019 and 2020. After 2021, it said, the amount of money going to individual farmers would depend on what efforts they make to improve the environment. The Campaign to Protect Rural England (CPRE) welcomed the plan. In common with some other environmental groups, it sees Brexit as a rare opportunity to make a greener land. It said:

'The new consultation phases out direct payments to farmers based on land area – which handed just 5% of the EU pot of money to farmers below average income – in favour of funding environmental improvements instead. It also fleshes out what the now familiar line of 'public payments for public goods' might mean: expect better air and water quality, healthier soils, more wildlife, lower greenhouse gas emissions, better access to the farmed countryside and greater protection for its ancient heritage.

'The planned approach post-2022 will be a new land management system that puts the environment first.'[22]

That sounds good. At first sight it seems absurd that the Common Agricultural Policy hands 95% of its money to the wealthiest farmers, although that is because they have the largest farms and therefore produce the most. But critics believe the CPRE is putting a highly optimistic gloss on our farming future. The CPRE itself recognises there is a catch:

'This might mean spending a little bit more on our food, but would that be so bad? In truth, we spend less than any other EU nation, except Luxembourg, per head on our food. Our obsession with cheap food has not done our health, our farming or our environment many favours, so this could be a turning point.'

The CPRE may be correct in all those assertions, although telling the British people that Brexit means paying more for food was not on the side of the 2016 Brexit campaign bus. Whatever the supposed benefits of 'spending a little bit more on our food' – as seen by the relatively wealthy supporters of the CPRE – that will, again, not be good news for the less well off, especially those who find themselves at the Trussell Trust's food banks. While many would welcome the proposed environmental benefits of Brexit for our farmland and food production, they are speculative and strongly disputed by some, because they may not survive ambitious trade deals with the United States and other countries.

The 'Easiest' Trade Deals in History

As part of the single market, British shoppers have benefited from low taxes on goods from other states within the European Union. We have also benefited from trade deals made by EU negotiators with other countries such as Japan and Turkey as a part of a separate arrangement, a customs unions. Leaving the EU customs union would leave behind all those ambitious trade deals with other countries which have taken years to conclude – unless British negotiators can somehow rapidly replicate years of work by Brussels.

Negotiations for a hugely significant EU-Japan trade deal began in 2013 and was only signed in 2018. The EU has a Customs Union agreement with Turkey. The British government discovered as late as February 2019 – apparently to its surprise – that neither the Japanese nor the Turkish trade deals could be 'rolled over' to benefit British consumers after Brexit. New rounds of British-Japan and British-Turkish talks would be necessary. This may be tricky. Japan, for example, may not be inclined to offer the UK's 66 million people the same deal enjoyed by the EU's 445 million people. If you eat Turkish olives, cheeses, figs, and dates, Japanese sushi rice and other products, you may see the prices rise.

When Britain leaves the single market, the UK government will be free to create a new bureaucracy for goods and services. In theory, that could mean increasing food imports from North America, Africa, Australia and other places, giving us access to cheaper food whose price was bumped up by EU tariffs. But despite the efforts of the International Trade Secretary Liam Fox, the big prizes in trade with these other countries or regions are mostly yet to be secured. The British government has been forced to recognise that one consequence of relying on EU officials for decades is that the UK's pool of negotiating talent has shrunk considerably. Future trade partners, including the United States, are well aware that Brexit offers great opportunity for its vast factory farms.

Beyond Liam Fox's fantasy prediction of striking the 'easiest' trade deal in history with the EU, any future agreements will be tough to negotiate. Britain is not, as we were also informed erroneously, 'holding all the cards.' In some cases the deck is stacked against us. Numbers count:

445 million EU citizens v 66 million Britons
325 million Americans v 66 million Britons

And the Trump administration has been explicit. President Trump is pursuing an 'America First' policy. It is abundantly clear from his ghost-written book, *The Art of the Deal*, that he is someone who does not see deal-making as a win-win with compromise on both sides, but as a zero-sum game producing a win for the United States and a loss for the other side. For American politicians there is no more sensitive industry than farming and what's known as 'agri-business.' Even if President Trump leaves office, the interests of this formidable lobby will not change. Agri-business lobbyists offer massive cash donations to Senators and Members of the US Congress in almost every state. Those Members of Congress in turn protect their own constituents whether they produce chicken in Arkansas, corn syrup in Kansas, or beef in Oklahoma. In post-Brexit Britain we need to be acutely aware of this.

How It Works

Broadly, the big American food producers demand that the UK dumps European standards and adopts standards acceptable in the United States. That would mean that while the butcher in Kent could still sell sausages and Whitstable salt-marsh lamb, our supermarkets would stock currently unacceptable American growth hormone-fed beef, chlorinated chicken and other products either not allowed in the European Union, or regarded as yucky by British consumers, or both.

So what are the facts? I've lived in the United States for many years and have eaten US chlorinated chicken with no ill effects. And in fact the European Food Safety Authority (EFSA) and the British Poultry Council agree that putting chicken carcasses in chlorinated water is not in itself unsafe. In 2005, EFSA concluded:

'On the basis of available data and taking into account that processing of poultry carcasses (washing, cooking) would take place before consumption, the panel considers that treatment with trisodium phosphate, acidified sodium chlorite, chlorine dioxide, or peroxyacid solutions, under the described conditions of use, would be of no safety concern.[23]'

But the catch is that 'the use of antimicrobial solutions does not replace the need for good hygienic practices during processing of poultry carcasses, particularly during handling…' Put simply, European health authorities do not believe chlorination itself is harmful, but consider it to be an unacceptable shortcut to better hygiene. Surveys (from slightly different time periods) suggests that the UK had only a sixth of American levels of salmonella food poisoning.

Whatever the science, it is the politics which rule in trade deals. American agri-business lobbyists have been open about all this. They insist that the price of a comprehensive US trade deal is for the UK to abandon EU regulations on genetically modified crops, antibiotics in meats, and some pesticides and herbicides such as glyphosate. All this would offer 'a once-in-a-lifetime opportunity'[24], according to the US National Grain and Feed Association and the North American Export Grain Association. A future US-UK trans-Atlantic market, they said, could 'act as a bastion against the EU's precautionary advances and its ongoing aggressive attempts to spread its influence around the globe.' The US Trade Representative (USTR) is also being lobbied to insist that the UK abandons geographic labelling rules – which ensure that Prosecco comes from Italy rather than, say, California, and a Cornish Pasty from Cornwall rather than Chicago.

Pork Barrel Politics

On 29 January 2019 the US Trade Representative's office held a 'Public Hearing on Negotiating Objectives for a US-UK Trade Agreement.' Craig Thorn of the National Pork Producers Council began his presentation by reminding USTR, the White House and all members of the US Congress just how powerful his organisation really is. He represents 60,000 'pork operations' in 42 states. A presence in 42 states means 84 US Senators out of 100 plus perhaps 200 members of the lower US House of Representatives will listen to the pork lobby. Some will receive (legal) campaign contributions. Many can be expected to vote accordingly.

Mr Thorn was blunt. Echoing the US grain lobby, he said that Brexit offers US pork producers 'a historic opportunity' because US pork 'is almost completely locked out of the UK and the rest of the EU.' There is a problem with tariffs but the real problem, he said, is to 'eliminate … five serious SPS barriers.[25]' SPS means 'sanitary and phytosanitary.' In everyday speech, the US pork lobby wants to remove EU health and safety measures from the UK.

Mr Thorn was particularly concerned because the EU bans 'pork produced with ractopamine,' and any future trade deal with Britain should insist we accept pork treated in this way. However the UK and EU are not alone in banning ractopamine. It is banned by China, Russia, the EU and many other countries around the world because, among other side effects, ractopamine can induce pigs to suffer from hyperactivity, trembling and broken limbs. Mr Thorn also insisted that the UK should change its mind on the use of pathogen reduction treatments, the US meat inspection system, and restrictions on antibiotics.

British experts are especially concerned about the use of antibiotics in animals reducing the effectiveness of antibiotics used to treat human illnesses such as E. coli or salmonella. In the US, astonishingly, 70% of all antibiotics are given to livestock, often prophylactically in the hope of preventing disease in crowded pens, rather than to cure illness in individual animals.

The World Health Organisation considers antibiotic resistance to be 'an increasingly serious threat to global public health' that could harm our and future generations. For many British medical and other experts this is a crucial issue, a trade deal breaker. In 2016, presenting a government review of the issue, Lord O'Neill, former chairman of Goldman Sachs Asset Management, said:

'One of our recommendations is to propose a major global awareness campaign because these things are being handed out like sweets. In countries like the US it's the case that there is greater use in agriculture than humans and that in itself is part of the problem...

'Within 35 years we might not be able to offer caesarean sections because you won't be able to have the drugs. You might not be able to have cancer treatments.'[26]

Even the North American Meat Institute, a producers' group, recognises widespread public concern about over-use of antibiotics in American farms.

US agri-business groups will nevertheless continue to lobby for American food standards to prevail in any UK trade treaty. The US Animal Health Institute and similar organisations say publicly that they will not support a future US-UK deal that does not address these demands. They are absolutely clear: no acceptance of US antibiotic use, no deal:

'We have noted, with concern, statements by certain UK officials indicating a desire to exclude the agricultural sector from the negotiation and an intention of maintaining regulatory harmonisation with the European Union. Should the UK adopt such policies, we see little basis for the negotiation of a bilateral trade agreement.'[27]

In considering a UK trade deal, Members of Congress and the White House are far more likely to take into account the views of American lobbyists, farm groups and meat processors than any British politician or health expert. Another contributor to the debate, Shawna Morris, speaking on behalf of the US milk and dairy lobby, revealed that members wanted to be able to label American cheese as 'parmesan' and 'feta.' Of course, all this is subject to negotiation, and perhaps British ministers will be able to ensure that high standards are enshrined in any future deal. But before we leave the subject, one further wrinkle in our food supplies comes with those who supply us with our favourite food – curry.

Let Them Eat Curry

Oli Khan is Secretary General of the Bangladesh Ca-
terers Association. In 2016, he advised his organisation's 150,000 members and their families from 12,000
restaurants to vote to Leave the EU. Mr Khan's reason-
ing was simple. By 2016, four curry houses a week were
closing in the UK. Rents were going up, so were business rates, and it was increasingly difficult to get good
curry chefs. Mr Khan was assured by Conservative MPs
and Leave advocates Boris Johnson and Priti Patel that
Brexit would result in immigration rules being eased
to allow in more staff from Bangladesh, India, and Pakistan. After the vote, however Mr Khan changed his
mind, because as he and his members discovered, 'these
false promises will not be kept any more.[28]'

In some ways things are even worse. The new
post-Brexit immigration rules, Mr Khan pointed out,
mean migrants coming from Bangladesh to work in a
curry house in Bradford or Brick Lane or Glasgow may
need to earn a minimum salary of £35,000 a year. This,
he said, is unaffordable to small family-run businesses.
Some curry house workers have already quit and returned to their country of birth, as a result, Mr Khan
said, of uncertainty about the future of the business and
'the rise in xenophobia.'

Just the Facts: Food, Foraging and Survival

A few years ago I was fortunate enough to go on a foraging course in Kent. One of the local experts showed
me how to find four species of seaweed to eat at low tide
on beaches under the white cliffs of Dover, wild garlic in

woodland in the countryside, and a variety of herbs and berries. This was topped up by a 'foraging' expedition to Deal market. Some British commentators joke that Britain can survive Brexit by 'digging for victory' as we did in World War Two. There have been scare story forecasts of empty supermarket shelves and hoarding. Neither scenario seems particularly likely without a 'no deal' Brexit (explored in more depth in *Chapter 8. No Deal*). Some dislocation caused by transport difficulties at ports may occur, but probably won't be a disaster. Nor, most experts agree, will Britain become self-sufficient in food. Our closely packed, heavily populated island will not go back to the land. Most likely, at some point, the European Union will come to an agreement with Britain on food because it is in both our interests to do so.

A post-Brexit world has some optimistic points. Some foods may become cheaper, particularly factory-farmed meat under a new trade deal with the US. (We will leave aside the conditions of production). Freed from the CAP's rules and subsidies, British farming may enter a new ecological golden age, where farmers are rewarded for green stewardship of their land though environmental subsidies.

On the other hand, it is equally possible, if not more likely, that a sluggish British economy (see *Chapter 3. Brexit, Our Jobs & Our Money*) will struggle to support green farming. Food standards in general will fall and, in order to compete with cheaper meat imports from the US and elsewhere, our countryside may become dotted with intensive sheds of dairy cattle and pigs that barely sniff the country air.

Unless British workers find a new-found desire to go picking berries in Kent, lettuces in Norfolk and rhubarb in Yorkshire, food may end up rotting in the fields. More probably a deal will be done to permit more EU workers, or more non-European labourers to come from Africa or Asia on short term visas.

The disruption of Brexit and the continuing weakness of the pound may well raise prices, for all of us and that means, almost certainly, unless more public money (funded by taxation) is redirected towards the poor, more people will experience difficulty feeding themselves and will be pushed towards food banks.

 ## 2. BREXIT & THE NHS

The most infamous yet successful political statement of recent times was written on the side of a bus belonging to the official Vote Leave campaign. It read: 'We send the EU £350 million a week.' Underneath was the vote-winning slogan: 'Let's Fund Our NHS Instead.'

The £350 million a week claim was corrected by statisticians, economists, journalists and others. Boris Johnson, then Foreign Secretary, baldly repeated it. This stubborn refusal by a senior government figure to accept a correction on a matter of factual significance prompted a highly unusual letter of rebuke. It came from Sir David Norgrove, chair of the politically independent UK Statistics Authority. He wrote to Mr Johnson:

'I am surprised and disappointed that you have chosen to repeat the figure of £350 million per week, in connection with the amount that might be available for extra public spending when we leave the European Union.

'This confuses gross and net contributions. It also assumes that payments currently made to the UK by the EU, including for example for the support of agriculture and scientific research, will not be paid by the UK government when we leave.

'It is a clear misuse of official statistics.'[29]

UK Statistics Authority officials are too polite to call people liars, but writing publicly about 'a clear misuse of official statistics' is about as close as it comes in British public life. Mr Johnson had the opportunity to apologise. Instead, he raised the stakes – and claimed the £350 million claim was too low. 'There was an error on the side of the bus,' he told voters. 'We grossly *underestimated* the sum over which we would be able to take back control.' (My italics.) He suggested that after Brexit the NHS would receive a boost of over £400 million a week.

Despite Sir David's dressing down, the promise of more money for the NHS resonated with the British public. It brilliantly encapsulated two strong feelings, and characterised how Vote Leave tapped into emotions.

Firstly, many British people feel the UK gives the EU a lot of money and receives little back in return. Secondly, voters love the NHS; it is a rock at the centre of British politics. Surveys show nine out of ten of us support the basic principles of health care for all paid for through taxation.

As many as two thirds of us would be prepared to pay more in tax for a better NHS. We love the NHS because of the quality of care, the fact that it is free at the point of use, the attitudes and behaviour of NHS staff, and the range of services and treatments available. But dissatisfaction is growing because of staff shortages, long waiting times, and a lack of funding.

Boris Johnson gives a speech in front of the Vote Leave battlebus during the referendum campaign in 2016

In its first report after the Brexit referendum, the King's Fund, a health care think tank, concluded that patients have become increasingly unhappy with the reality of the services they actually receive. Non-urgent appointments at my local GP surgery – and almost certainly yours – take longer to obtain than they used to. A routine cholesterol or smear test might be delayed for days or weeks. The same is true for non-urgent elective surgery in over-stretched hospitals; ask anyone who has a hip or knee problem.

And we know that every winter there is likely to be some kind of NHS beds crisis, with a knock-on effect on other parts of the service. To put this in context, repeated winter bed crises are simply unknown in, say, Germany. The reason is that Germany has more than eight hospital beds per 1,000 citizens. France has six per 1,000. The UK has fewer than three beds per 1,000.

The 2016 Brexit promise 'Let's Fund Our NHS Instead' was therefore extremely attractive because every winter our newspapers and TV programmes are full of stories about our excellent, super-efficient and relatively inexpensive health care system being pushed beyond its limits.

Some leaders of the Leave campaign, including Nigel Farage and the Conservative MEP Daniel Hannan, believe they can improve health care in the UK by taking a completely different tack. They have publicly supported privatising all or significant parts of the NHS. At a meeting of UKIP followers in 2012, Mr Farage was very clear:

> 'I think we are going to have to move to an insurance-based system of health care. Frankly, I would feel more comfortable that my money would return value if I was able to do that through the marketplace of an insurance company, than just trustingly giving £100 billion a year to central government and expecting them to organise the health care service from cradle to grave for us.'[30]

This old-time American health care religion has been proselytized in different terms by Mr Hannan and others. So, Brexit and its impact on health care is defined by growing public dissatisfaction with the NHS, and a promise of more money from Mr Johnson – while Mr Farage and Mr Hannan think the system could be improved by more privatisation.

The over-arching question is whether our families will enjoy better funded NHS care in Brexit Britain. Since the optimistic claims made on the side of the Brexit bus, health care professionals have become gloomy about what will happen. In an opinion poll of NHS doctors and nurses in 2018, about 64% said they thought the NHS would get worse after Brexit, compared with just 7% who thought it would get better.[31] So what is the truth? First, let's look at the NHS's finances.

The NHS and Money

When the NHS was launched in 1948, it had a budget of £437 million. That's roughly £15 billion in today's money. But for 2017-18, the actual NHS budget was seven times higher, £108 billion. Spending has been driven up by two main factors: a rising population, and rising expectations. There are more of us (and we live longer) and we want new treatments.

Unsurprisingly, given the vast sums, UK health spending takes up almost 10% of GDP. Is that value for money or would we be better off looking at another model? In the United States (where health outcomes are generally worse) health spending takes 17% of GDP. Put another way, in Britain we spend £2,892 on health care for every person in the UK, while the cost for each American is £7,617. Health care costs are the single biggest source of personal bankruptcy in the USA. In 2017, the Commonwealth Fund think tank studied the efficiency of health care systems in 11 advanced countries[32] and put the UK squarely at the top, with the US at the bottom. The ranking was:

1. UK
2. Australia
3. Netherlands
4. Norway
5. New Zealand
6. Sweden
7. Switzerland
8. Germany
9. Canada
10. France
11. United States

This is testament to the NHS's resilience and extraordinary efficiency after the longest financial restrictions in its history as a result of government policies since the 2008 stockmarket crash. British people still get excellent world-beating health care, on the cheap. Among the good health care options, only New Zealand, Norway and Australia spend (a little) less than the UK does as a percentage of GDP. But here's the catch. While there is some private health care provision in the UK, health spending on the NHS comes from taxation. And taxation relies on the performance of the British economy. Every authoritative projection for the British economy shows that as a nation we will be poorer after Brexit *(see Chapter 3. Brexit: Our Money & Our Jobs)*, which means that unless politicians cut the budgets of other departments like education and defence and funnel that money into the NHS, health spending will be lower after Brexit that it would otherwise have been.

Despite the bluster on the bus, then, the NHS is likely to be squeezed by Brexit – because the economy is already being squeezed. In 2019, two economists at the London School of Economics, Josh De Lyon and Swati Dhingra, found clear evidence of a slowdown in the UK since the EU referendum: 'GDP growth has slowed down, productivity has suffered, the pound has depreciated and purchasing power has gone down, and investments have declined.' In a blog, they warned:

'The UK has slipped from having the highest growth rate in the G7 before the vote, to the lowest now. This suggests GDP growth has held up likely as a result of international trends, but it is showing weakening internal trends. Productivity has also suffered. The negative signs of economic health are confirmed by the outcomes in productivity stagnation. Output per worker has continued to be stagnant since the referendum. Worryingly, the gap between output per worker in OECD countries and the UK has widened since the referendum.'[33]

Much of this was as a result of Brexit uncertainty. Many economists refuse to forecast growth or the likelihood of recession in a post-Brexit Britain because the picture is too unpredictable, but the weight of informed opinion is gloomy. The Bank of England growth forecast by 2019 was slashed to 1.2%, the lowest since 2009 when the economy contracted after the financial crash. The outlook for 2020 was 1.5%. All this puts the UK near the bottom of European growth projections.

Even if NHS spending does take a bigger share of our GDP after Brexit, the likely outlook even for optimists is that health care for all of us might obtain a larger slice of a shrinking cake. And doing that, with an expanding population, is unlikely to maintain the levels of service we are already receiving, which many of us consider to be unsatisfactory (even though we love the NHS as a whole).

Paying for Drugs

Other NHS funding pressures have already come into play. The post-referendum drop in the value of the pound has made importing pharmaceuticals more expensive. Some stockpiling or hoarding has taken place. Until a final deal is negotiated with the EU, Brexit may disrupt the importation of medical necessities not manufactured in the UK. Precautionary preparations for such difficulties began in 2018. In December that year, the Health Secretary, Matt Hancock, announced: 'I've become the largest buyer of fridges in the world, I didn't expect that.'

The fridges were necessary to stockpile medical supplies. Hancock was both optimistic and cautious. 'If everybody does what they need to do then I have confidence that we can have the unhindered supply of medicines and medical devices and the other things that the NHS needs,' he said. 'Now, that relies not just on the Government and the NHS doing what they need to do, it also relies on other organisations like pharmaceutical companies for example.'

In fact, Mr Hancock did not buy fridges. An NHS insider familiar with the project said that civil servants took out contracts to rent refrigerated warehouses, so that they could stockpile medical supplies in the event of a no deal Brexit (see *Chapter 7. A No Deal Brexit* for more on that). That prospect receded but what began as the promise of £350 million a week extra to the NHS suddenly transformed into the reality of emergency spending on refrigeration. The money could have been spent on your local hospital or GP surgery, but Hancock was right to be prepared.

In February 2019, weeks before Britain was first supposed to leave the EU, Dr David Wrigley, a highly respected GP and deputy chair of the BMA Council, tweeted:

Dr David Wrigley @DavidGWrigley · Feb 19
Every day as a GP I get the message back from the pharmacy (after prescribing) that x, y or z medication is not available. Happens more & more but almost impossible to say whether it's due to Brexit or drug suppliers diverting supply to maximise profit (poss to due Brexit too!)

    ○ 12   ⟲ 56   ♡ 62   ✉

Dr Wrigley's tweet was amplified on social media by other doctors, pharmacists and patients who complained about shortages of painkillers, anti-depressants and other medicines. Eighty medicines were placed on the 'shortage of supply' list for England that month, meaning the Department of Health agreed to buy them at a premium. Four months earlier, the list contained 45 products. The Royal Pharmaceutical Society said 'a massive shortage and price spikes' was attributed to a number of causes, but in particular it blamed stockpiling caused by Brexit.

One of the strengths of the NHS is that it is the biggest buyer of drugs in the world. This is good news for Britain. As the worldwide pharmaceutical industry's biggest customer, the NHS can drive a hard bargain. I have attended numerous medical conferences including in San Francisco, Paris and London, at which some of the largest big pharma corporations privately (and sometimes publicly) complain that the NHS drives down prices not just in the UK but also in the EU, by setting a low benchmark. Even if such prices are supposed to be confidential, customers in other health care systems are anxious to find out what the NHS pays. If they do, they use that baseline as ammunition in their own pricing discussions.

Even so, the cost of medicines has been rising above inflation. Estimated total NHS spending on medicines in England has grown from £13 billion in 2010-11 to £17.4 billion in 2016-17 – an average of 5% a year, well above inflation. All the indications are that Brexit will increase the drug costs paid by the NHS, not simply because of stockpiling or threatened shortages or even the fact that the cost of medical services is greater than inflation. Just the fall in the pound makes many prescription and non-prescription drugs more expensive, simply because they are not made in the UK.

Where Do Medicines Come From?

Many treatments could be mentioned here but let's stick with just two: insulin and molybdenum-99.

First, insulin. Diabetics must inject insulin in order to control blood glucose. One in 10 of us over the age

of 40 has diabetes. An astonishing one in 20 of all pre-
scriptions written by GPs is for the disease. The NHS
currently spends 10% of its budget on diabetes treatments – and diabetes is becoming more common. As
the journal Diabetic Medicine puts it:

> 'In total, an estimated £14 billion pounds is spent a year
> on treating diabetes and its complications, with the cost
> of treating complications representing the much higher
> cost. The prevalence of diabetes is estimated to rise to 4
> million by 2025.'

Even without factoring in Brexit, and potentially
higher import costs for insulin, the NHS is predicted
to spend 17% of its entire budget on diabetes by 2035.
If left unchecked, this bill could bankrupt the health
service, according to Barbara Young, chief executive
of Diabetes UK.

Brexit, however, puts the treatment of diabetes under further strain still, because no insulin is made in
the UK. It is imported from Germany, France and
Denmark. In theory, as with food supplies, if we
have problems importing insulin from the Continent
we could order supplies from elsewhere. In the case
of insulin 'elsewhere' realistically means the United
States. But suddenly switching the source of even
common drugs from the EU to the US is not as simple as shopping at Tesco instead of Lidl. Diabettech,
the Diabetes and Technology website, explains the
problem succinctly:

'99.7% of insulin prescribed in the UK is imported from the EU. If the UK health care services were to try and come to an agreement with Eli Lilly US for import from the US, it would be new ground, a completely new set of contracts, and an interesting challenge in respect of logistics, so it's not the immediate panacea that has been suggested.'[34]

An 'interesting challenge' is what British diplomats call a bureaucratic nightmare. Perhaps those refrigerated warehouses will become useful after all, depending – yet again – on the lengthy post-Brexit negotiations. But as we will see throughout this guide, whether Brexit actually happens or not, and whatever the detailed negotiations actually come up with in the end, the 2016 Brexit vote itself has already dislocated our country and made life more expensive in myriad ways.

If importing and exporting food products seemed complicated, imagine the paperwork necessary for pharmaceuticals and medical supplies.

The Expert View
Brexit has given and continues to give UK government ministers, civil servants, health professionals and medical researchers nightmares about shortages, bottlenecks, and bureaucracy. As with food supplies, changing decades-long trading relationships means devising whole new sets of rules, regulations, standards and customs checks. We have had years of frictionless trade in medicines as part of the single market. Brexit means that's over. According to the authoritative health care think tank the Nuffield Trust, in the worst case the 37 mil-

lion items of medicine imported from the EU could – depending on final trade negotiations – face up to 44 new checks, requirements and controls:

'Selling medicines to the NHS would suddenly require people within the UK checking batches and holding an official marketing authorisation. Customs checking and declarations will also be required...

'As well as the delays they directly cause, the sudden introduction of these barriers would create two further problems. The first is the disruption of supply chains. Business models that rely on, for example, testing in the Netherlands of UK manufacturing products would no longer be legal. Those that rely on input materials being provided 'just in time', with no space or funds for stockpiling components, will struggle not to interrupt supply. The second is the risk of queuing and chaos at ports and borders.'[35]

Where medicines are concerned, the margin of error is small. Work by the British Retail Consortium suggests that meat importers could face an irritating but do-able wait of a few days at ports for refrigerated French chickens or Danish pork. But health experts point out that just two or three days is a period as long as the half-life of molybdenum-99. Molybdenum-99 is used to produce technetium-99m, which is given to patients so that the patterns of the radiation it produces can be used to scan the skeleton, heart and other organs for cancer or damage. All molybdenum-99 is imported. Most of it comes from the Netherlands, Belgium, Poland, and the

Czech Republic. While you might hope a crucial radio-isotope could skip the lorry queue, this assumes a level of order that seems far from certain.

The Royal College of Radiologists has said it may have 'no choice but to prioritise' which patients receive cancer treatments. To be clear: this is a life or death decision. At least one in three of us will suffer from cancer at some time in our lives, more like one in two. Every one of us knows someone who has had or will suffer from the disease. The difficulties of obtaining molybdenum-99 might seem technical, but early diagnosis of tumours increases survival rates.

For diabetics, cancer patients and others, the government has said that in the worst cases supplies could be flown in. As an emergency measure, the UK could even waive almost all regulatory and customs checks for medicines from the EU. Even so, we are so bound into our trade with Europe that the Association of British Health Tech Industries gave the Parliamentary Health Select Committee a stark example of another real problem:

'Becton Dickinson, the largest supplier of needles and tubes for blood collection in the NHS, manufactures its products in Plymouth before they are transported to Belgium for product checking and distributed back to the UK.'

For UK medical companies which shuttle goods under 'frictionless trade' for product checking in the EU, these vital health supplies could be held up on the other side of the Channel simply because there might be less urgency there about patients in the UK. If you already think you are waiting too long for a routine blood test, Brexit may not be the answer you are looking for.

Of course, common sense and goodwill may prevail. But the legal, health and political implications could be severe. The first UK patient who dies because of our inability to source enough molybdenum-99 or insulin will have a grieving family demanding answers from the government, and perhaps complaining to the newspapers or in the courts. Moreover, those who once sang the praises of trading on World Trade Organisation rules (which would govern our trading under a no deal Brexit) would soon find that any special deals to avoid checks for EU medicines would have to apply to all other trading partners. So, we would have to abandon all checks for those drugs from all countries. It is difficult to imagine that many British patients or their doctors would wish that to happen.

Staff Shortages

Let's cheer us ourselves up. Let's assume that Britain enjoys a smooth Brexit transition, leading to a quick EU trade deal and that Matt Hancock's fridges – or enormous warehouses – will be required only for milk for nurses' tea. There remains another post-Brexit concern which is already a chronic NHS problem and at the heart of the things most of us dislike about the NHS. That is long waiting times caused by staff shortages and lack of facilities, especially in winter.

As we are increasingly aware, this is exacerbated by a lack of social care, especially for our ageing population. So what will be the impact of Brexit on the people who treat you at your GPs surgery, in care homes and in hospitals? We trust doctors, nurses and midwives more than any other professions. Our life is quite literally in their hands. But there is a big question mark over whether post-Brexit Britain will find the qualified staff we need to maintain and improve the NHS.

Brexit and a Hospital Near You

If you have to get sick, Homerton University Hospital in Hackney in north east London sounds like a good place to find yourself. It's typical of many big city NHS hospitals – 500 beds, 11 wards, six main operating theatres, an intensive care unit, maternity, paediatric and neonatal wards. It serves a diverse population admitting 60,000 patients a year, seeing a quarter of a million outpatients, and delivering 6,000 babies. Homerton's Care Quality Commission rating is 'Good.' When it comes to emergency services or medical care, including care for the elderly, it is rated 'Outstanding.' The only weak spot noted by the CQC has been maternity and gynaecology, which needed improvement.

The most recent headcount of staff numbers at Homerton offers a picture similar to that in many other big city hospitals, and of the NHS in general. In 2015, of the 3,500 total, 347, 10%, came from the EU27. The hospital, like the entire NHS, is proud of its diversity.

After the 2016 Brexit referendum one of the hospital workers, consultant urologist Junaid Masood, put a picture on Facebook which went viral on social media under the headline 'We are Europe!' Mr Masood's team consisted of three scrub nurses from Spain, a German consultant

Urologist Junaid Masood makes a point about European co-operation

anaesthetist, an Irish radiographer, a Greek urology specialist registrar, plus Junaid Masood, who described himself as British Pakistani. The caption reads: 'Today we have been hard at work improving people's lives! This is what our friends from Europe do for the NHS.'

A local paper[36] republished the picture and quoted one of the Spanish nurses, Marina Seminario, aged 26, from Malaga, who had worked at Homerton for three and a half years. 'I particularly enjoy working with so many colleagues from around the world,' she said. 'If I went back to Spain it is this that I would miss most. I am happy here and hope that I can stay in the future.'

This portrait, with its motivated staff from different countries and of different backgrounds, will be familiar to big city hospital patients all over the UK. But by 2018 it became obvious to hospital managers that preparations for Brexit were making staff recruitment even more difficult.

Nursing

Nurses make up the largest professional group in UK hospitals. Following the Brexit vote many EU nurses in the UK returned to their home countries or went elsewhere. New staff have proved hard to find. Homerton University Hospital NHS Foundation Trust said it was concerned 'at the highest levels' that 'continuing uncertainty' over the future of EU workers post-Brexit was having a negative impact on staff, and 'new recruits from Europe have dried up'. A trust spokesman said it was 'increasingly difficult' to recruit nurses, despite a recruitment drive in India and the Philippines. Currently, 150 nursing posts are unfilled, representing 11.5% of the total in nursing and midwifery.

Just as with food banks, it is unclear how much of these staff shortages can be attributed to Brexit and the loss of EU workers, and how much to the policy of 'austerity' which has affected public services since the Conservatives took office in 2010.

But nationally the NHS's performance does seem to be worsening. Those waiting for more than four hours to be treated in NHS Accident and Emergency units in England rose from 353,617 in 2010 to 2,778,687 in 2018. And behind every statistic is a human story. To take one relatively minor example, an anecdote, but a telling one – a friend of mine living in a middle sized town in south-east England fell and broke her collarbone. It took two and a half hours for the ambulance to arrive. We cannot directly connect that event with any single cause. But what we can conclude, since this is what health professionals themselves say, is that the NHS that most of us love is getting worse. Brexit isn't helping, at least so far.

Brexit Bonanza and Going Global for Staff

Currently the NHS employs around 1.7 million people, 1.2 million of them in England. To state the obvious, lack of money means lack of staff. Lack of staff means longer waiting lists for operations and treatment, a worse service, and lower care standards. Short staffing in the wards means your mother may not be checked for dehydration at the right moment, or the tests on your child may be delayed until a harassed but caring staff member can finish with another patient.

Official figures showed that in 2018 the NHS in England was already missing at least 100,000 staff, including 10,000 doctors and 40,000 nurses. Three health care think tanks projected that on current trends the gap between staff needed and the number available after Brexit in 2020 could soon hit nearly 250,000, leaving one in six posts unfilled. The three think tanks, the King's Fund, Nuffield Trust, and Health Foundation, warn:

'If the emerging trend of staff leaving the workforce early continues and the pipeline of newly trained staff and international recruits does not rise sufficiently, this number could be more than 350,000 by 2030.'

The shortages, they said, stemmed from 'an incoherent approach to workforce policy at a national level, poor workforce planning, restrictive immigration policies and inadequate funding for training places'. The report does not mention Brexit. But the anecdotal evidence of EU staff leaving and not being replaced is striking. Some health care experts do make a clear connection with events since the Brexit referendum, and their NHS projections go far beyond Project Fear towards Project Terrifying.

Brexit Nursing Shortages and Social Care

Writing for the Nuffield Trust, Professor Martin Green, Chief Executive of Care England said that Brexit was 'having an impact on our ability to both recruit and retain our EU staff.' Professor Green offered a clear insight as to why this was happening: money. He said:

'Many commentators have said this is about people not feeling welcome within this country, but in my view it has far more to do with the slide in the value of the pound. At one time it was very advantageous for European citizens to work in the UK because the exchange rate between the pound and the euro was such that it really did make financial sense to work here. Now that there is almost parity between the two currencies, it is easier for workers to find employment on the mainland of Europe, enabling them to have much easier access to their friends and families at home.'[37]

Social care has been hit, too – damaging an important industry. About 400,000 people live in adult social care homes. More of us live longer and unfortunately more of us may also suffer from dementia. Finding caring people prepared to work in the 11,000 adult care homes throughout the UK, to wash, feed and change the incontinence pads of the elderly, has never been easy. It is not well paid work.

In 2018, a report by the National Audit Office revealed that around half of UK care workers received £7.50 per hour or below, equivalent to £14,625 annually, just above the National Living Wage of £7.20 an hour. According to the NAO, the vacancy rate in the 1.34 million jobs in the adult social care sector in England was 6.6%.

Analysis by the Nuffield Trust calculated that the UK will be short of as many as 70,000 social care workers by 2025-6 if net migration of unskilled workers from Europe is halted or seriously disrupted after Brexit. (In their reliance on relatively cheap labour from the EU, care home providers are much like British farmers.) The Trust argues that 'either substantial migration of such staff from the EU will have to continue after Brexit, or wages in UK care homes and home care agencies may need to rise to attract more home-grown staff.'[38]

The upshot of all this is quite obvious. Those of us who will live out our last days in care homes, or who have parents or relatives in that situation, will find that after Brexit there will be fewer willing underpaid, overstretched EU workers willing to clean our bedpans and give us a sponge bath. If these EU workers are to be replaced, it will most likely be from poorer countries outside Europe, including India, Pakistan, China, the Philippines, Nigeria, Ghana, and other nations in Africa. Once again, this may not be the result some Brexit voters were hoping for. The alternative – raising wages – would put more strain on people paying for relatives' care and already struggling local authorities.

Global Britain – Again
There is another consequence of Brexit which complicates labour shortages both for social care (mainly for el-

derly people) and hospital services. The NHS and social care providers need to consider what will happen to the estimated 190,000 British over-65 pensioners currently living in other EU countries, predominantly France and Spain. Within the EU they receive health care under the EU reciprocal 'S1' scheme. This has already become a political issue in Spain. As the London correspondent of a Spanish newspaper told me:

> 'We send you our young people to England to work; you send us your old people to die.'

If many of those 190,000 British pensioners in the EU decide their health requirements demand they return to the UK in the event this S1 scheme benefit is withdrawn after Brexit, or because they feel less welcome, or because their pound sterling pensions do not stretch so far, then the cost to the NHS is put at a further £1 billion.[39] That is around twice the amount that the UK government currently reimburses to other EU states for the care of the British elderly. In other words, UK taxpayers would have to find an extra £500 million net.

Future NHS planning therefore may involve senior managers figuring out how to cope with losing significant numbers of young EU-born care, nursing and other medical staff (such as those at Homerton Hospital) while gaining tens of thousands of more elderly and costly Britons who have returned from abroad. The calculations here are stark. Around 900 extra hospital beds, equivalent to two new Homerton hospitals, would be required if all 190,000 British pensioners returned from the EU. Even if new hospitals and extra beds could be found, the shortages of key medical, nursing and care staff would become even more acute, putting pressure on other services and care for younger patients.

The Nuffield Trust puts a price on the increased cost of medicine post-Brexit:

> 'There is also a risk that the NHS will no longer have access to as wide a supply of medicines at as good a price if the UK leaves the EU's medicine licensing system. The extra cost could exceed £100 million.'[40]

The Trust dismisses the phoney promise on the Brexit bus, noting that 'all sides in the Brexit debate agree that the £350 million per week figure used during the EU referendum will not materialise,' but adds optimistically that when the UK stops paying its EU membership fees, it 'could give the NHS additional money for one or two years.'

The key phrases here are 'could' and 'for one or two years.' And then what? Two options present themselves, neither of which is immediately attractive. If the idea of the NHS is to continue in post-Brexit Britain, then it will require significantly more public money than at present (that is, more from taxpayers) as well as probably yet another significant re-organisation. The second possibility, currently politically unthinkable but most definitely being mooted by some of the most ardent proponents of Brexit, is to 'reinvigorate' the NHS by allowing in more private investment especially from American health care firms. We will move on to that possibility in a moment.

The Long Term Health of the National Health Service

But first, one other factor, again not directly related to Brexit, compounds the pessimism about the long term future of the NHS. The current shortage of 40,000 nurses will be made even worse because nursing and midwifery have an ageing demographic. More than half the nurses in the UK are older than 45. A third of midwives are already over 50. They can retire at 55. The Royal College of Midwives estimates there is already a 3,500 shortfall in the midwifery workforce in England. The Royal College of Paediatrics and Child Health says one in five paediatric trainee positions and one in four more senior posts are vacant. Mental health services have 20,000 vacancies in England – one in 10 funded posts.

Staff from overseas made up about 14% of nurses, 22% of GPs and 35% of hospital consultants. Some 7% of nurses and 9% of doctors are from EU or EEA countries. A surging number of recruits from the EU has now gone into reverse. In September 2017, the number of EU nurses and midwives leaving the UK register rose by 67% year-on-year. In the same period, the number of new EU/EEA nursing recruits choosing to work in Britain fell by 89%.[41]

Project Fear and Project Fact: the Missing Nurses

To repeat one key theme: stories about the ill effects of Brexit are routinely dismissed as Project Fear by the most ardent Brexit advocates. They argue that in future somehow plenty of UK nurses will be trained and non-EU nurses, midwives, doctors and others will be attracted to the UK. This is possibly true. Medical staff from the EU will undoubtedly still train and work in the UK. But the rows over Brexit, the uncertainty, the divisions in our country, the hatred and racist speech at the edges of our political life, the sense of xenophobia unleashed by some of our citizens all spoil our image abroad. And so do the hard facts about NHS pay and the value of the pound. So let us conclude on the survival of the NHS with some further thoughts from those who have spent their lives in health care, the Cavendish Coalition. The Coalition brings together 36 organisations across health and social care and commissioned a report from the National Institute for Economic and Social Research to consider how Brexit would affect staff shortages. It makes grim reading.

It suggested that on top of more than 40,000 existing vacancies for nurses we can expect perhaps another 10,000 vacancies to appear as a result of Brexit. The report was particularly concerned by specific shortages in problem areas because EU/EEA nationals are 'more likely to work in specialties and locations with weak domestic supply.'

Danny Mortimer, NHS Employers chief executive, called the figures 'startling' and said the impact of further losses of such staff 'should be taken extremely seriously' by those negotiating with Brussels.

'The health and social care sector is deeply reliant on talented colleagues from across Europe and the rest of the world so it is deeply disheartening to see these projected workforce gaps at a time of rising demand for services.'

The Lancet View

A month before Theresa May's original Brexit deadline of 29 March 2019 the medical magazine *The Lancet* offered a review of various Brexit scenarios, representing the thinking of the majority of clinical experts in the medical profession.[42] It can be summed up by the first sentence:

'All forms of Brexit will negatively impact the UK National Health Service, but the prospect of a No-Deal Brexit presents by far the worst scenario, with negative effects on the health care workforce, NHS financing, availability of medicines and vaccines, sharing of information and medical research.'

Whatever kind of Brexit Britain had, there was 'little evidence … that the UK is prepared for *any of the eventualities.*' (My italics.) *The Lancet* findings are worth quoting in some detail, because they confirm and underline some of the difficulties we have already mentioned:

'Recruitment and retention to the health care workforce represents a major challenge post Brexit. The Withdrawal Agreement provides reciprocal arrangements and mutual recognition of professional qualifications up to 2020. But, no provisions for health care workers have been made in the Backstop or Political Declaration. And, under a No-Deal Brexit, the Immigration White Paper proposes a minimum salary threshold of £30,000 per year which could seriously limit immigration of many health workers to the UK.'

In simple terms, as they stand, government proposals will not allow into the UK many of the low-paid workers on which the NHS depends.

Then the report focuses on the problems ahead for British people living or travelling to the EU (dealt with in more detail later in this book):

> 'Under the Withdrawal Agreement, reciprocal health care arrangements (eg via the European Health Insurance Card, EHIC) would remain but only until 2020 as there is no mechanism to continue them subsequently, although some limited bilateral agreements may be possible with time.'

The answer here would appear to be that those of us who wish to travel in the EU will require private health insurance, rather than the reciprocal arrangements we have become used to. (Ill health while travelling is dealt with in more detail in *Chapter 5. Brexit & Travel*)

Then, money from European sources for the NHS – something under-reported in the UK media – will also dry up:

> 'Access to capital financing for NHS infrastructure via the European Investment Bank would be negatively impacted in all scenarios. As one of the largest areas of public expenditure, any negative impact in the UK economy will put additional pressure on NHS financing, and the UK has already seen a slower rate of economic growth than if it had remained in the EU. The idea that Brexit will bring a 'deal dividend' has been described as not credible by the Treasury Select Committee.'

As for medical supplies, 'the continuity of legal provisions will secure supply chains for medicines, vaccines, medical devices and equipment until 2020.' Nevertheless 'despite Government reassurance of contingency plans in place, shortages are likely because stockpiling arrangements cannot cope more than a few weeks, proposals that doctors offer 'best alternative medication' can be distressing for patients, and some products (such as radioisotopes) cannot be stockpiled.'

The European Medicines Agency has now quit its offices in London, making the UK less attractive for global pharma to launch new medicines – 'potentially meaning launch dates up to 24 months later.' That means new and possibly life-saving treatments which in the past have come to the UK first, could be delayed for up to two years. You can imagine the public outcry when British parents read in their newspapers that a treatment which could save their child's life is available in Germany, Austria and France, but not the UK (until, perhaps, after the death of their son or daughter).

Finally, the post-Brexit legislative task ahead is so immense that parliament will have to pass several massive new pieces of legislation and up to 600 statutory instruments in short order. That means other important work such as new legislation on improved social care has suffered prolonged delays.

The result, *The Lancet* concludes, is a dire assessment of and ambitions for a renewed Global Britain as it would affect our international reputation, public health and our environment:

'Any form of Brexit will also harm the UK's European and global leadership role in health. Membership of the European Centre for Disease Control is not mentioned in the Withdrawal Agreement, and while the Political Declaration mentions global collaboration on public health, it does not reference European collaboration. UK laws on air pollution, workplace health and safety, and tobacco trade derive from EU law.

'With the UK having failed to meet standards on air quality, there is concern that the UK might use Brexit to roll back some of these measures.'

Professor Martin McKee, from the London School of Hygiene and Tropical Medicine and co-author of *The Lancet* article, says:

'Some people will dismiss our analysis as 'Project Fear'. But …. we need to move beyond slogans. We have set out the problems in detail, based on the best available evidence. If others disagree, then they owe it to the British people to say why. It just isn't good enough to keep saying that 'something will work out' without any details of exactly how.'

We can, in other words, trust politicians to tell us about how good health care will be after Brexit, or we can trust those doctors and other health professionals into whose hands we place our lives and those of our families.

Trade Deals, 'Death Panels,' and the NHS

The last big unknown about Brexit and our health – as with many other issues – is how far the UK will need to come to terms with the requirements of other countries outside the EU in order to negotiate comprehensive trade deals. This, as the former US Defence Secretary Donald Rumsfeld used to say, is a Known Unknown. As with our food supplies after Brexit, the US Trade Representative is under enormous political pressure from the American pharmaceutical and health care industry for Britain to open up more to US products and services.

For a flavour of how the NHS is seen from the White House, President Trump tweeted in 2019: 'The Democrats are pushing for Universal Health Care while thousands of people are marching in the UK because their U(niversal) system is going broke and not working.' President Trump clearly does not think much of the NHS. And like American pork producers, the US health care industry sees a huge post-Brexit opportunity in Britain. Others see an existential threat to the NHS.

The pharma industry lobby group PhRMA, which represents US drug makers such as AbbVie Merck and Novartis, said it wants a US-UK trade deal to remove the barriers to access it currently faces in the UK. In particular, America's big pharma lobbyists criticise UK price controls and the current NHS drug approval system known as NICE (National Institute for Health Care Excellence).

As someone who has worked in the US for many years I was stunned to hear NICE repeatedly described on US TV's Fox News as a 'death panel.' Fox's American viewers were told that British 'death panels' decide whether a sick person should or should not receive a particular medicine in our 'socialized' system. Of course, far from being a 'death panel' NICE is a group of health care experts who try to work out whether a new treatment is effective enough for the NHS to spend money on. But the death panel story – which peaked when President Obama was trying to change the US health care system against the wishes of big private health care lobbyists – is worth bearing in mind. It helps explain how the UK is seen or at least characterised in the minds of some Americans.

The US position has long been that the British cap on the price of drugs is too restrictive and the NICE process too rigid. The loudest voice in the Brexit debate, Nigel Farage, has tended to keep quiet in more recent times about his views that the NHS should be replaced by an American-style private insurance system. But others are not so reticent. Right-wing thinkers have already begun making trans-Atlantic plans for the new post-Brexit Britain.

Their views have been voiced by the Initiative for Free Trade (IFT), a libertarian think-tank founded by the Conservative MEP and leading light in Vote Leave, Daniel Hannan, and American counterparts in the Cato Institute. The Cato Institute is bankrolled by major American political donors to right-wing low-tax small-government causes, the Koch family. In 2018, the IFT published online plans for 'the ideal UK-US free trade deal.'[43] The authors argued for a deal 'more liberalising than any other free trade agreement in the world.' That would include removing tariffs, but also removing EU regulations on hormones in meat, pesticides, chemicals in cosmetics, GM foods based on 'precautionary' principles. The deal also says: 'Health services would benefit from foreign competition though we recognise change to existing regulations would be extremely controversial.' The plans include allowing American health care companies to run British hospitals, and appear to chime with Nigel Farage's statements about moving from the taxpayer-funded NHS to a private insurance based system. During his June 2019 visit to Britain, President Trump insisted that the future of the NHS would be 'on the table' as part of any trade deal, 'absolutely.' The backlash against these remarks stretched from Labour to Conservatives, all insisting that the NHS was not for sale. Within hours Mr Trump backtracked and said: 'I don't see it being on the table.' Perhaps readers will trust President Trump on this. But since the US health care lobby is among the most powerful in Washington and managed to derail many of President Obama's most ambitious plans for health care reform, it is impossible to believe that the future of the NHS is not on the agenda from the American side, whatever the protestations of some British politicians.

Of course, if the NHS thrives after Brexit and the government finds the extra £400 million or more a week, then our health care system will fix the Brexit challenges of restricted funding, staff shortages and long waiting times. But from years of dealing with NHS leaders and staff, I can confirm that the biggest concern within the health service is not some sweeping change. It is fear of a long, slow financial squeeze which makes our NHS health care more and more unsatisfactory. In these circumstances, more patients will opt to pay for private medical care and, slowly, we may decide that it is not worth the taxes we pay to fund a post-Brexit NHS. Then we may vote for parties who will offer to put a failing NHS out of its misery.

It hasn't happened so far. We still love the NHS. But avoiding a lingering death through loss of staff and loss of confidence will be one of the key challenges of Brexit.

3: BREXIT, OUR JOBS & OUR MONEY

Brexit has profoundly affected our money, our family finances, our jobs, our economic security and our future prosperity since 2016. The impact has been largely, if not overwhelmingly, negative. The drop in the value of the pound is only part of the story, though it has been noticeable to any British person going on a foreign holiday. The actual or looming departure of major manufacturers, entrepreneurs, financial services companies and other employers from the UK has done lasting damage to the UK economy, to jobs, businesses, and to our capacity to innovate.

But in what follows there is one important caveat. When a factory in the Midlands or a high street shop in Glasgow closes, a financial service company moves out of London to Holland, or a small business relocates to Austria, there are usually many causes. I spend a great deal of time in business and investment conferences, including for major accountancy firms and their blue chip clients, investment fund managers, property and building companies and manufacturing industries. In all these sectors Chief Executive Officers (CEOs) and Chief Investment Officers (CIOs) always consider an array of factors before investing, dis-investing or moving a company's operations to another country. They also plan what they intend to do before setting a time limit on when they intend to do it. That is simply common-sense. None of the dozens of CEOs and CIOs with whom I have discussed Brexit would have done what the United Kingdom has done – set a certain date to complete the biggest transformation of their businesses before working out what that transformation would involve and how to achieve it. In pressing the button to start Brexit and complete it by 2019, the former prime minister Theresa May did something no business leader would contemplate. That historic error is at the root of many of the economic problems we now face. No business would decide to scale a mountain by a set date without first agreeing which mountain they were about to climb.

Brexit therefore has become a major factor in the self-inflicted economic and industrial damage being done to the UK economy. The picture constantly changes and different organisations collect data in slightly different ways, but stripped of political rhetoric, as we will see, the facts all point in the same unhappy direction – to Britain being poorer after Brexit than otherwise we would have been.

Some of the most striking statistics come from the Brexit Jobs Lost Index, which is collated by a Facebook account BrexitWrecksIt. It states that Brexit has so far cost at least 200,000 jobs. The index is transparent, listing individual job losses and its methodology. Firstly, it's clear that it takes a very broad view, including for instance job losses where the employer's business has been significantly affected by sterling's devaluation, 'either immediately through rises in the cost of imported inputs or later by inflation passed on by those who were so affected.' It also includes job losses caused by austerity cuts (since without Brexit 'austerity would have been lifted instead of deepened'), and all cases where jobs are moving abroad. It also includes redundancies announced by companies affected by potential trading barriers thrown up by leaving the EU or whose business has slowed significantly after the vote without any other obvious explanation.

Between the referendum of June 2016 and 8 April 2019, the Jobs Lost Index puts the total UK jobs lost due to Brexit at 218,839. Estimates of annual wages lost ran to £6.27 billion, money which we could have spent on food, clothing, cars, and other purchases with the usual 'multiplier effect' through the economy. There was also an annual tax loss to the government from foregone income tax and national insurance of £1.8 billion. That could have gone on health, schools, defence and other matters which touch our daily lives. According to the website SmallBusinessPrices.co.uk, job losses by region were:

- Midlands: 22,162
- London: 19,507
- South West: 10,943
- Wales: 10,866
- North East: 10,401
- Scotland: 5,647

- North West: 3,989
- South East: 3,798
- East of England: 2,663
- Gibraltar: 1,000
- Southern England: 870
- Northern Ireland: 462
- Nationwide/unknown: 126,531

Then, the worst hit sectors of the economy:

1. Automotive: 48,112
2. Transport: 30,394
3. Food & Drink: 28,615
4. Finance: 15,152
5. Construction: 13,644
6. Clothing: 8,544
7. Aerospace: 4,154
8. Agriculture: 3,100
9. IT: 2,505
10. Hospitality 2,450

Among the biggest jobs losses were:

Hitachi/Horizon: 8,500
Tesco: 6,222
Poundworld: 5,000
Jaguar Land Rover: 5,000
Deutsche Bank: 4,000
Rolls Royce: 4,000
Vauxhall dealerships: 3,800
Sainsbury's: 3,400

It is clear that several businesses on the list have been hit by specific problems which arguably have little if anything to do with Brexit. Retailers such as Sainsbury's have to deal with the rise of web shopping or budget competitors. Car manufacturers such as Jaguar Land Rover know that consumers have switched from diesel to petrol or electric cars. But Brexit has played a significant part in the decision to move some businesses elsewhere or fail to invest in new plants. Car-makers who export to mainland Europe, engineering firms with European supply chains and globally-facing banks have been especially hard hit. All rely heavily on being able to trade with ease in the EU.

When Jaguar Land Rover, Nissan and Honda all announced the movement of car production from Britain it came after months of weighing up key factors. Executives will have considered changes in consumer tastes in the car market, emissions standards, the unpopularity of diesel cars, the vagaries of the Chinese economy and so on, as well as the implications of Brexit. But Ralf Speth, chief executive of JLR, was clear.[44] He warned that Brexit could kill off thousands of jobs in the British car industry. Underlining the nature of modern 'just in time' supply chains, Dr Speth said:

'Just one part missing could mean stopping production at a cost of £60m a day. That is a huge risk. We depend on free, frictionless, seamless logistics.'

When Boris Johnson challenged Dr Speth's expertise on this matter he was told by Nick Ferrari on LBC that the boss of Jaguar Land Rover would know more about car manufacturing than a politician with a chequered career as a journalist. Mr Johnson replied with customary modesty: 'I'm not certain he does.'

A clear majority of business leaders, investors and economists say the Brexit vote and the ensuing uncertainty have been bad for the British economy, discouraging investment and encouraging companies and entrepreneurs to move elsewhere. But let us begin with the good news.

The Good News

The Bank of England's fears that the 2016 Brexit vote would trigger a recession and mass unemployment were unfounded. Despite notable Brexit-related lay-offs, more jobs have been created in the economy in the subsequent three years. In the first three months of 2019, for instance, the rate of unemployment ticked down to 3.8% – the lowest since 1974. It was 4.9% in June 2016.

There are a couple of caveats, though. Firstly, employment tends to lag behind output in reflecting economic changes. Howard Archer, chief economic adviser at EY ITEM Club, stated that the ongoing 'uncertainties' were persuading companies to hire people to fulfill orders rather than making big investments in plant and machinery. He said:

'Employment growth has undoubtedly been lifted by businesses preferring to employ rather than commit to investment given current heightened uncertainties. Employment is relatively low cost and easier to reverse if business subsequently stalls.'[45]

Secondly, employment in Britain is 'relatively low cost' and flexible, giving businesses the ability to scale workforces up and down quickly depending on demand. While some workers in the 'gig economy' delivering parcels or takeaways may welcome the chance to set their own hours, others feel that their position is precarious and powerless. About 6% of workers are thought to be on 'zero hours' contracts which guarantee no hours[46], and others work fewer hours than they would like. Low pay and low job security are common in Britain. Nonetheless, a job is a job, and employment is almost certainly better than no job.

And the UK has much lower unemployment than in many EU countries. Across the Eurozone, unemployment is about 8%. In Italy it is 10%, France 9%, and in Germany 3%. Joblessness among under 25s is disgracefully high in southern Europe – in Spain around 30%, or one young person in three. But to re-state the obvious, Britain's low unemployment rate in 2019 comes while we are members of the European Union.

At any rate, as a result of this tighter jobs market, employees have been able to bargain successfully for higher wages. Wage growth in the UK by the end of 2018 hit 3%. Bigger wage packets began to repair some of the falls in living standards in the 'lost decade' of austerity from 2008.

Britain as a Magnet for EU Workers

Back in 1973, before the UK joined the Common Market, Britain was often called the 'Sick Man of Europe.' London had lost about a quarter of its population from 1939 to the early 1990s. Membership of the EU and Margaret Thatcher's reforms changed all that. London, in particular, attracted economic migrants from all over the world and began to rival New York as the world's most important financial centre. Compared with the sclerotic Eurozone economies of southern Europe, Italy, Greece, Spain, Portugal and to an extent France, jobs have been easier to find in Britain. And the relative openness of borders under the single market has made Britain a land of opportunity for decades. We have successfully attracted most of the extra workers employers needed, from those who work in the fields and farmlands to factories and finance houses and your local hospital.

Whatever voters may 'feel' about immigration, the facts about how new workers benefit the economy are clear. Repeated studies calculate that EU citizens who work in the UK bring value. They put in more than they take out. Oxford Economics estimates that the average EU migrant contributes £2,300 a year more to the public purse than the average British adult, suggesting 'a net contribution of £78,000 to the exchequer over their lifespan in the UK'.[47] The study calculated that this boost to the UK economy was like the government receiving an extra 5p in the pound on income tax, which means we all benefit from lower taxes and higher public spending than would otherwise be possible. Those who 'feel' EU migrants are a drain on the economy are simply wrong. We may 'feel' the Earth is flat but the facts on its shape, like those on the net benefit from EU migrants to the economy, do not always accord with 'feelings.'

EU vs non-EU for Business

We are a country which is rightly seen as good for business, but so are some other countries within the Eurozone. The Netherlands, for example, has lower unemployment even than the UK and a higher GDP per head, a key measure of prosperity. The Netherlands' currency is the euro. After China and the US, Germany is the world's biggest exporter. Economic success or failure is to do with the business culture, and that culture has brought success in the UK, Germany and the Netherlands. Italy, Spain, Greece, Portugal and France have higher unemployment largely as a result of their own national policies, structural problems and cultural preferences.

A CEO I know who ran for many years a company in southern England with more than 5,000 employees worldwide told me his only big regret in business was opening an office in Paris. He found it impossible under French labour laws to get rid of one troublesome employee. As a result, when he expanded his French workforce he employed talented French people – but in England. The UK's labour laws allowed him to fire workers fairly easily, so as he put it, the risk of hiring a wrong 'un was minimal.

The Eurozone itself is a mixed blessing for its members. It works wonderfully for Germany and the Netherlands and gives southern European countries the benefit of a stable currency. But that means they cannot (as Italy did for decades) make themselves more competitive by repeatedly devaluing. In the 1970s, the Italian lira was a joke; British holidaymakers found themselves counting out lire in the thousands to make even a minor purchase. Britain has prospered within the EU because, ironically, we really have been able 'to have our cake and eat it.' We have joined the world's biggest single market but kept our post-Thatcher flexible labour market (good for bosses, bad for some workers), and a strongly inventive entrepreneurial culture. We have also maintained our economic independence by opting out of the euro, which allows us to devalue our currency to make our exports more competitive. The austerity years programme known as quantitative easing can be interpreted as doing just that.

The Not So Good News

Few things in British political life are more contentious than the economic costs and benefits of being in the EU. The Leave and Remain campaigns in 2016 were both guilty of factual distortions and selective use of statistics. The Leave campaign and its proponents bombarded us with fanciful promises of 'sunlit uplands' and the 'easiest' trade deals in history once we escaped the 'straitjacket' of Brussels. The Remain campaign produced scare stories and dubious predictions of an immediate recession if we dared contemplate Brexit. Political wishful thinking on both sides took over from expert assessments. In 2016, Leave campaigners constantly talked about the genuine hardship many families were facing. But they did not dwell on the fact that much economic hardship (evidenced by the rise of food banks) was rooted in the UK government's own austerity programme. The Remain campaign similarly did not blame austerity, in part because one of its leading figures, the then

Chancellor of the Exchequer, George Osborne, created austerity. Mr Osborne was reduced to telling everyone how much worse things would get if we voted for Brexit. But this was effectively dismissed by the Leave campaign with two words. As it turns out, Project Fear has turned into Project Fact, and the economic dislocation already caused by the Brexit vote may prove to be minor compared to more severe dislocation later.

One reason, however, that Leave was so effective in dismissing the gloomy economic forecasts of 2016 is that economics is sometimes referred to as a dismal science and its forecasts as jokes. One of the most respected Keynesians, Paul Samuelson, famously quipped that the stock market has predicted nine of the past five recessions. George Bernard Shaw joked that if you laid all the economists in the country end to end they would never reach a conclusion. And the Leave campaigner and Cabinet minister Michael Gove touched a nerve when he asserted that the people of Britain 'have had enough of experts.'

Nevertheless, most experts and mainstream economists have reached clear conclusions on how Brexit will affect – and has already affected – UK jobs, prices, tax revenues, and your money. Taking into account inflation, the drop in the pound, wage rises and other factors, as a nation we are poorer than we would otherwise have been without the economic shock of the Brexit vote, and any form of Brexit is likely to make us poorer still.

What follows are some of the facts which back up that gloomy conclusion.

The Big Picture: Brexit Has Made Us Poorer Already

Since the referendum, the UK's economic growth has slowed while the G20 group of leading nations have powered ahead. In 2015, UK GDP grew at 2.3%. In 2018, it fell to 1.4%. According to Gertjan Vlieghe, a member of the Bank of England's Monetary Policy Committee, since June 2016 the British economy has lost 2% of expected GDP – which works out at £40 billion a year, or £800m a week[48]. In short, Britain has lost every week more than twice the £350 million a week extra we were promised for the NHS.

The poorest, as usual, suffer most. The Centre for Economic Performance at the London School of Economics calculated that the immediate effect of the 2016 Brexit vote was a 1.7% spike in UK inflation. In money terms, that means the Brexit vote alone cost the average household £7.74 per week in higher prices, £404 per year. Higher inflation reduces the positive effects of any growth of wages. The CEP concluded that the impact of the post-referendum hike in prices 'is equivalent to a £448 cut in annual pay for the average worker,' or the loss of one week's wages.[49] Different workers in different regions of the UK have inevitably suffered in different ways. The richest region – London – has suffered least. Poorer areas – Scotland, Wales and Northern Ireland – 'are worst affected.'

Many middle class or wealthy people may have barely noticed such price rises. But for those earning a low wage, especially in poorer areas of the country, the immediate aftermath has been acute pain, especially after a decade of government-imposed cuts. One development, as we have seen, has been the rise in food poverty and the need for food banks. In 2018, Philip Alston, the UN rapporteur on extreme poverty, visited the UK and took 300 submissions and heard stories from dozens of people in person. His final report in 2019[50] was scathing:

'Although the United Kingdom is the world's fifth largest economy, one fifth of its population (14 million people) live in poverty, and 1.5 million of them experienced destitution in 2017... Close to 40 per cent of children are predicted to be living in poverty by 2021.'

After meeting the UK government, Alston concluded that planning for how Brexit would hit the poor was 'an afterthought.' A falling pound and lower economic growth led to one conclusion, he said:

'Almost all studies have shown that the UK economy will be worse off because of Brexit, with consequences for inflation, real wages, and consumer prices.'

With Brexit we were told we could have our cake and eat it. Instead the truth is that the cake – whatever we choose to do with it – is smaller than it otherwise would have been.

High Finance

Brexit, however, has been good for some. Money is to be made in times of uncertainty, especially by those who can speculate on wild swings in prices or exchange rates. In 1987, William Rees-Mogg, editor of *The Times* and father of the ardent Brexiter, Jacob Rees-Mogg, co-authored a book which some describe as the bible of 'disaster capitalism.' As the title suggests in *Blood in the Streets – Investment Profits in a World Gone Mad*, Rees-Mogg senior explained that while economic upheaval might upset most of us it could benefit speculators. He was right.

Prior to the referendum in 2016, the hedge fund manager Crispin Odey donated almost £900,000 to UKIP and other campaigns in favour of leaving the European Union. He then made a financial killing by betting (wisely) against the UK economy when, against almost all predictions, Leave won the vote. The pound fell dramatically. The day after the vote, Mr Odey said:

> 'There's that Italian expression – 'Il mattino ha l'oro in boc-ca' (the morning has gold in its mouth) and never has one felt so much that idea as this morning.'[51]

Since then, Mr Odey's business interests have made more money from the continuing uncertainty for the UK economy, our jobs, pension investments and savings. As he put it: 'Bad days tend to be good days for us.' By mid 2018 Mr Odey was again betting against British companies doing well. He was reported to have 'shorted' or bet against a rise in value of 'telecoms firm Talk-Talk (£7.5 million) shopping centre owner Intu (£40 million), upmarket property developer Berkeley Group (£45 million), car dealer Lookers (£2.5 million) and a string of retailers, including department store Debenhams (£17 million).' At the same time he was 'bullish' (optimistic) about investments in France, Germany and the US. *Financial Adviser* magazine said he was investing 'in such a way that he will profit if investor sentiment turns against the country (the UK.)'[52]

You may think it curious that someone who spent so much money backing a campaign that told us how good Brexit would be for Britain should make so many bets that would pay out if Brexit hurt British businesses.

Mr Odey is not the only prominent Brexit campaigner to look abroad after the vote. Somerset Capital Management, a hedge fund company co-founded by Jacob Rees-Mogg, set up a new fund in Brussels-friendly Ireland. Mr Rees-Mogg insisted the fund's launch had 'nothing whatsoever to do with Brexit.'[53]

Industry experts, however, have told me that any financial company in post-Brexit Britain needs a foothold in the EU. The need for some firms to set up a new base outside the UK was expressly acknowledged by Lord Ashcroft, another Brexit advocate, when he picked his favourite member state. While saying that Britain remained 'the best location for nearly all UK companies', the former Conservative Party chairman recommended Malta on account of its sunny climate, 'wonderful' quality of life and low crime rate. He wrote: 'I believe that Malta represents the best destination for ambitious UK firms that must have a post-Brexit presence in the European Union.'[54]

Another business leader who insisted Brexit would be great for Britain, Sir James Dyson, has moved his company's headquarters from Wiltshire to Singapore following the October 2018 Singapore-EU trade deal.

It's worth repeating that after Brexit, Britain does not have a trade deal with the EU despite having an EU land border in Ireland. Singapore does have a trade deal, despite being on the other side of the world. Dyson said it wanted to be closer to its key Asian markets.[55]

In all of this, readers will make up their own minds whether publicly advocating Brexit as good for Britain while shifting money or offices abroad is merely good financial stewardship or hypocrisy. Or perhaps both.

Why We Have Not Had Enough of Experts

More recently Crispin Odey has suggested publicly that Brexit will not happen at all. This comment should carry just as heavy a health warning as those promising a Brexit Britain will be blessed with riches. I got an expert view in early 2019 when I chaired a financial services conference of economics and investment experts in Manchester and took part in other similar conferences in London, Hampshire, and Edinburgh. The participants at all these events handled billions of pounds of investments, including perhaps your company or private pension fund, your ISAs or investments (if you are lucky enough to have them). They discussed how to manage risk in an uncertain post-Brexit Britain and focused on political mismanagement and instability, questions about where the UK was in the economic cycle, inflation, the prospect of companies pulling out of the UK, international difficulties including a slow-down in China, the unpredictability of the Trump administration, and so on. All of these factors (and more) play into investment – and dis-investment – decisions. The big brains present included the Chief Executive Officers and Chief Investment Officers and other leaders from some of the biggest investment companies in the UK. They had differing views on how some things would turn out, but most agreed on the key areas.

At the Manchester conference a clear view came from Emiel van den Heiligenberg of Legal and General Investment Management. Brexit, he said, has already caused irreversible problems for the UK economy:

> 'We shouldn't kid ourselves… The transfer of financial activity to Frankfurt or to Paris is actually happening; car production moving from here in the UK to Europe or to emerging markets is actually happening – and it's not coming back even if we get a deal on Brexit. Some of the rot has already set in – and we can't reverse it.'[56]

Guy Monson of Sarasin & Partners, an asset manager, broadly agreed there was an air of Brexit-inspired pessimism but he suggested it might be misplaced in the long run:

> 'I am going to be controversial and say that I am rather an optimist for the UK. But I am concerned about the challenges it means for all of us sat here today. I have sat in asset allocation meetings in Europe and of the hated assets currently, one of things most investors dislike are all things British.
>
> 'I wonder then if in fact the UK then goes from pariah to something of a safe haven. Currency is cheap; our employment mar-

kets are extraordinary; and asset markets are incredibly undervalued. I think the international investor therefore will come back to the UK.'

David Jane of Miton Group stole the show in Manchester when he put the past three years of uncertainty (and the inner strength of parts of the UK economy into perspective) with a personal anecdote.

'I was speaking to a friend recently who owns a small restaurant chain in London and one which has enjoyed huge growth thanks to growth in home deliveries. He asked me: 'You're in financial markets: what about Brexit; what's going to happen?'

I said: 'I haven't got a clue,' before adding: 'But what will you do if there is a Brexit deal?'

He said: 'Mate, I've got such high demand for what we're doing, I'll have to open a new factory.'

Then I said: 'Well, what will you do if they kick the can down the road and postpone Brexit?'

He said: 'Mate, I'll have to open a new factory, because I've got such an increase in demand.'

Then I said: 'Well, what will you do if there's no-deal.'

He said: 'Mate, I'll have to open a new factory.'
(Loud laughter in the room.)

I said: 'Why haven't you opened a new factory already?'

He said: 'Because of Brexit.'

There was more laughter at the punchline. The story brilliantly summed up how political and economic uncertainty fosters business inactivity. The businessman in the story reached the same conclusion whatever happened with Brexit – but he avoided or postponed doing anything about that decision because he did not know precisely what would happen with Brexit. As economics, it may seem daft. As business psychology, it is impeccable.

One further Brexit story shows how the same 'fact' can be interpreted or misinterpreted to suit political convenience or prejudices. In February 2019, Norway's sovereign wealth fund, the world's largest, announced it was increasing exposure to British companies, property and bonds. Brexiters welcomed the news as a wholehearted endorsement of Brexit. This was a mis-reading, deliberate or accidental, of the true position. Norway's Government Pension Fund Global has a time horizon of 30-plus years. Yngve Slyngstad, its chief executive, pointed out that buying more UK assets was therefore a very long term vote of confidence in Britain.

The Norwegians have probably made a sound investment. UK asset prices are currently low because of the slide in the pound and the uncertainty following the Brexit vote. As our optimistic investor Guy Monson explained, foreign investors have been 'avoiding all things British' but 'currency is cheap; our employment markets are extraordinary; and asset markets are incredibly undervalued.'

Investors make money through buying low and selling high. If there were ever to be a milder or no Brexit, the pound will 'shoot up like a rocket', a staunch pro-Brexit campaigner told me.

Nobody Knows Anything. Or Do They?

William Goldman, the famous Hollywood screenplay writer once quipped that in movie-making 'nobody knows anything' – you never really know if a movie will be a hit or not. It's a great phrase and may be true of Hollywood but it's not quite true of other fields of human endeavour. Well-informed financial experts know a great deal – that's why they are rich and mostly successful at investing other people's money. But not even prime ministers have been able to predict the outcome of Brexit. Businesses are used to swimming in choppy seas, but Brexit planning has involved thinking about everything from the tide going out or a tsunami rushing in. From numerous discussions with financial and economic experts, if there is a broad consensus of opinion, it looks something like this:

1. Uncertainty will continue. Select any of the preferred cliches – the usual one is that we are 'in uncharted waters.'

2. The pound may have bottomed out. (But one financial expert told me that in his opinion a no deal Brexit could cause a further big drop in sterling.)

3. As Emiel van den Heiligenberg noted, Brexit has already damaged Britain's business reputation, with employers planning to leave the UK and relocate some or all of their operations to the EU 27. At every business or finance conference I have attended in recent months over coffee and networking sessions the finance experts talked about examples of companies they knew personally which had left or were considering leaving the UK.

At one conference a CIO drew my attention to an online report in *Business Insider*, in November 2018, which listed some organisations which had gone or were going, with Frankfurt being considered a 'winner' as a new location.[57] The list is worth reproducing, because, it shows how easily high finance can shift operating bases across national borders.

• British banks are hedging their bets and deploying resources out of Britain and into the EU. Barclays won permission to shift assets worth £166 billion ($216 billion) to its Irish division. Barclays is set to become Ireland's biggest bank. HSBC, Europe's biggest bank, has shifted ownership of many of its European subsidiaries from its London-based entity to its French unit.

• Other types of UK finance are acting too. Europe's biggest repo trading venue, called BrokerTec, is moving from London to Amsterdam, shifting a $240 billion a day repo business away from the UK. More than 100 UK-based asset managers and funds have applied to the Irish central bank for authorization in Ireland.

• US bank giants Goldman Sachs, JPMorgan, Morgan Stanley, and Citigroup have moved 250 billion euros ($283 billion) of balance-sheet assets to Frankfurt because of Brexit. Bank of America is spending $400 million to move staff and operations in anticipation of Brexit, and is trying to persuade London staff to move to Paris.

• Banks from other EU states are also shifting assets and staff. France's BNP Paribas, Credit Agricole, and Societe Generale have opted to transfer 500 staff out of London to Paris. Germany's Deutsche Bank is considering shifting large volumes of assets to Frankfurt as part of its Brexit plan.

• Swiss banks are moving, too. UBS has chosen Frankfurt for its new EU headquarters. Credit Suisse is moving 250 jobs to Germany, Madrid, and Luxembourg among other EU 27 countries as well as $200 million from its market division to Germany. And in December (2018) Credit Suisse told its wealthiest clients to extract their money from the UK before Brexit.

• Australia's largest bank by assets, Commonwealth Bank of Australia, has set in motion plans to base around 50 staff in Amsterdam, and has applied for a banking licence in the country. Other Australian lenders Macquarie, Westpac, and ANZ are also in talks to relocate operations to Dublin and continental Europe.

Politics and economics are, of course, utterly intertwined. The politics of Brexit has caused economic dislocation, and the economic dislocation is creating new political flashpoints, including intense feelings in Scotland about the decisions taken in Westminster. At a conference in Edinburgh, I was told potential investors were deterred from making major investments in the UK because Westminster politics was seen to be 'in crisis,' 'inept' and 'incompetent.' Some were worried by a freak combination: a weak prime minister had been coupled with a weak and business-unfriendly leader of the opposition in Jeremy Corbyn. Edinburgh, a financial centre in its own right, where Remain won a resounding victory in 2016, found itself being pulled out of the EU and unable to compete for new finance business because Belgium, Germany, Ireland, and the Netherlands were more attractive since they remained pillars of the EU single market. This was helping to make the case for Scottish independence, one major investor said, even though he personally was against it.

It is, however, worth noting that the European Securities and Markets Authority and its British equivalent, the Financial Conduct Authority (FCA), have agreed a degree of stability for financial markets. They have signed a memorandum of understanding to ensure funds marketed in the European Economic Area (which includes the EU) will still be able to be managed in the UK and vice versa. This is useful for those in financial services and the City of London, but it is 'temporary' and 'for a limited period.'

Sayonara

The Japan-UK love affair began in the 1980s. Margaret Thatcher welcomed Japanese businesses, telling them that Britain could be their high-skilled 'gateway to Europe' since we were part of what was to become known as the single market. English was also the one language the often mono-lingual Japanese tended to learn at school.

In total, Japan has created almost 150,000 jobs in the UK since the 'gateway to Europe' promise in the 1980s. At the beginning of 2019, Britain had up to 1,000 Japanese businesses, including Toyota, Mitsubishi, Panasonic, Fujitsu, Sony, and massive Japanese banking groups such as Mizuho, Nomura and Daiwa.

In 2016, however, Japan issued an uncharacteristically frank warning about Brexit. In a stunning 15-page report it said that companies would leave the UK if Brexit negotiations were unsatisfactory. The report expressed deep concern about the fate of automobile manufacturers and pharmaceuticals. For Japan's medicine makers the report said the EU's European Medicines Agency (which subsequently relocated to Amsterdam in 2019) was crucial to the UK's high-tech research appeal.

Carmakers were vulnerable because they feared trade tariffs and cross-border bureaucracy with levies being imposed twice – 'once for auto parts imported from the EU and again for final products assembled in the UK to be exported to the EU – which would have a significant impact on their businesses.'

In 2017, standing beside his then British counterpart, Theresa May, the Japanese prime minister Shinzo Abe said 'the fact that after the decision on Brexit, Japanese companies are continuing to make new investment into the UK … shows the profound trust that Japanese companies have toward the British economy.' That, however, changed when the ineptitude of Brexit negotiations in Brussels sent shock waves through boardrooms in Tokyo.

Just as the negotiations between London and Brussels were being mishandled, another gate to the big European market opened for Japan. In 2019, a Japan-EU trade deal guaranteed Japanese businesses direct access to the EU single market – without having a base in the UK. Worse, post-Brexit Britain was told that it could not simply 'roll over' existing trade deals made by the EU including ones with Japan, Turkey, Algeria and other countries.

The Japanese Brexodus swiftly followed. Electronics manufacturer Panasonic said it was moving its European HQ from the UK to the Netherlands. Japanese banks Nomura and Daiwa began setting up EU operations in Germany. Hitachi, Sony, Toshiba, Honda and many others are planning to employ fewer British workers in future. Hitachi has abandoned its plans for the next phase of Britain's nuclear power industry at Wylfa Newydd on Anglesey and at Oldbury-on-Severn in Gloucestershire. Toshiba quit a similar project in Cumbria. Honda executives denied the end of production at Swindon with the loss of 3,500 jobs was Brexit related – but in the past they had publicly expressed concerns about the impact of Brexit. While all kinds of different reasons were cited for the loss of faith in the UK, Japan's ambassador in London was clear. After the Japan-EU trade deal was signed in February 2019, he said:

'If the lack of predictability (in the UK) continues, businesses will find it very difficult to continue operating or investing.'

Brexit, to put it simply, is a job-killing machine.

Job Losses: Hello 'Lloyds of Belgium' and the 'Brussels Broadcasting Corporation'

Japanese companies are only part of the jobs Brexodus. South Korean investors, who until 2019 were big in the London property market, pulled out of multi-million pound deals including plans to buy the UK headquarters of Credit Suisse at Canary Wharf (£460 million).

Some big British names sought to mitigate the effects of Brexit on their businesses, too. The insurance and re-insurance market Lloyds of London announced it had received regulatory approval from the National Bank of Belgium to establish an insurance company in Brussels. The BBC was planning to set up shop in Brussels, too.

Other big manufacturers and banks have said they are slimming down or pulling out – again, citing a variety of reasons, though some specifically mentioned Brexit. Among them were: Airbus, Deutsche Bank, JP Morgan, Goldman Sachs, P&O, HSBC, Philips, and Bank of America. As the senior chairman of investment bank Goldman Sachs, Lloyd Blankfein, put it pointedly in a tweet:

Beyond the big names, many small and medium enterprises are already leaving or planning how to do so. The British Chamber of Commerce warned that frustrated firms were shedding jobs and investment. Dr Adam Marshall, its Director General, said:

'As our global competitors get sharper and more strategic, Britain is still mired in indecision and uncertainty. Drift and lack of direction have real-world economic consequences, brought home to many of our communities not just by high-profile business closures, but by the quiet and growing loss of contracts, investments and jobs.'

The accountancy firm EY has a 'Brexit Tracker' following 222 companies. As of June 2018, a third, 75, had 'publicly confirmed, or stated their intentions, to move some of their operations and/or staff from the UK to Europe.'

The Institute of Directors (IoD) warned that 29% of firms in a survey of 1,200 members believed Brexit posed a significant risk to their operations in the UK and had either moved part of their businesses abroad or were planning to do so. Edwin Morgan, the IoD's interim director general, said[58]:

'While the actions of big companies have been making headlines, these figures suggest that smaller enterprises are increasingly considering taking the serious step of moving some operations abroad. For these firms, typically with tighter resources, to be thinking about such a costly course of action makes clear the precarious position they are in.'

Beyond recitations that all this was somehow connected to 'the will of the people,' some Brexiters maintain that a UK 'free' from the 'straitjacket' of EU rules and regulations could move towards being a highly productive low-tax economy. A cut in corporation tax would undoubtedly increase the prospect of foreign investment. But there is a catch in even this seemingly straightforward plan. Panasonic Europe's chief executive Laurent Abadie pointed out in an interview with *Nikkei Asian Review* that if the UK lowered corporation tax after Brexit we could be considered by other countries to be a tax haven.

Mr Abadie concluded that that designation could lead to Japanese and other foreign companies with UK bases being penalised by tax laws at home, and forced to pay more tax there. Corporation tax reductions would also provoke retaliatory measures from the EU and elsewhere.

For those of us who do not run a business, or who do not invest in one – that is, most of us – leaving the European Union adds up to fewer jobs, a less attractive economic outlook, a diminishing of Britain's reputation for business competence, and ultimately a country which has decided to make itself poorer than it would otherwise have been.

Brexit and House Prices

One final area of finance which touches many of us directly is house prices. UK house prices, especially in the south east of England, have been high, putting home ownership out of reach of many ordinary people. Aspiring homeowners may be pleased if a post-Brexit economic slump cuts prices (although existing homeowners will not be so happy). So what has happened to the affordability of housing? According to the Land Registry UK, house prices rose steadily from £215,127 in July 2016, the month after the referendum, to a high of £231,936 in August 2018. They have fallen every subsequent month, hitting £226,798 in April 2019 – still higher than before the referendum, but on a firm downward trend. Rightmove reported that it was taking properties an average of 70 days to go under offer in 2018, compared to 67 days at the same time in 2017.

One veteran estate agent who has seen markets bounce up and down for years told me that, in simple terms: 'People aren't moving unless they have to.' Another agent with decades of experience said simply: 'Why would anyone sell or try to buy the biggest asset in their lives in a climate of uncertainty like this?' No panic, no drama, but what appears to be a slowdown. Good for home buyers, not good for homeowners.

Economic Survival

When it comes to surviving Brexit, no doubt British inventiveness and hard work will overcome all the problems outlined throughout this chapter. But it is worth remembering that Brexit is not a natural problem; a plague of locusts eating our economy. It is a man-made political decision with what appear to be some calamitous consequences for the prosperity of these islands. I've dwelt on the financial sector here because it is highly significant, because investors are necessary to put money into good ideas which create jobs, and because so many finance houses employ forward-thinking business people who have talked to me off the record about what the future holds. But I want to conclude this chapter on surviving Brexit with one final expert.

Sir Mark Boleat is an important figure in the City of London. He was director general of three big British financial organisations: the Building Societies Association, Council of Mortgage Lenders, and the Association of British Insurers. For five years until May 2017, he was chairman of the City of London policy and resources committee, which tries to attract international businesses to London.

Sir Mark expects that the more than £70 billion that the financial services sector pays into the public purse in tax is about to start declining.[59]

He believes the total costs incurred by the financial services industry in preparing for Brexit 'already exceed £10 billion – a huge waste of resources.' The financial services industry 'will, subject to sorting some transitional issues, be fine after Brexit and, indeed, is ready to cope with 'crashing out', but a significant proportion of it will no longer be in the UK, and that proportion will increase over time. Sir Mark said:

> 'It is unquestionable that Brexit will cause a massive loss of jobs and tax revenue as business shifts from London, even though London will retain its status as a major international financial centre. To some this may be a price worth paying – although I suspect that many of those saying this will not be the ones paying the price. I cannot see how it can be a price worth paying for the people of Britain.'

4: BREXIT & OUR CHILDREN'S EDUCATION

In the 1990s Marisol, a Spanish woman in her early 20s came to Britain because there were no job opportunities in her home town of Valladolid. She felt she was doomed to become part of that lost generation of unemployed young Spaniards, where one in three cannot find employment. The UK offered Marisol a fresh start. She found minimum wage work at a kindergarten where it had been difficult to recruit local British workers. She supplemented her income by teaching Spanish in private conversation lessons. Then she became a school teaching assistant, worked hard and eventually qualified as a Spanish teacher, married an Englishman and settled down in the UK. She has children of her own now, in school and doing well. For her, Britain was the land of opportunity.

At first sight Brexit looks as if it will affect education modestly – perhaps deterring just a few ambitious migrants like Marisol with specialist language qualifications of little interest to most monolingual Brits. British schools and educationalists believe otherwise. They foresee big problems ahead.

We need to begin by understanding that the term 'British schools' has no real meaning. Scotland's education system has always been set apart from those of England and Wales, with different exams and a different university system. Wales is also different in some respects from England. Northern Ireland, with its Catholic Church school tradition, is unique, too. Morever, even within the English and Scottish systems, Eton and Fettes are clearly very different institutions from local state schools, and in some areas grammar schools still exist. It's a patchwork system, but educationalists across the UK at all levels have serious concerns about how Brexit will change schools and higher education at a time when we are told we will need to exploit the advantages of 'Global Britain.'

Language teaching is obviously part of that, and it is in trouble. In 2019, a BBC investigation found that foreign language learning was at its lowest level in UK secondary schools since the turn of the millennium, with German and French falling the most. In some areas of England the number of pupils taking GCSE language courses since 2013 has dropped by up to 50%. If we are truly preparing for a Global Britain, that is not in evidence in the priorities of many of our educational establishments. Beyond what some parents may see as the niche area of language teaching, education specialists see two other major risks from Brexit.

The first is unquantifiable, but real and important. Britain is a brainy country with a worldwide reputation in education. We have some of the best universities in the world. These universities and our top schools are at the heart of British 'soft power,' our image and influence abroad. Foreign countries send to our schools and colleges young men and women who will become future presidents, prime ministers, world-renowned scientists and business leaders. Political leaders from India, Iran, Ireland, Malaysia, Pakistan, Portugal, Syria, Turkey, the US, and many others have studied here. Pupils and university students who study in the UK mostly go home and tell their country that our country is a good place to be, a good place to do business.

The second Brexit risk is most definitely quantifiable. It's money. The money Britain earns from international students at universities supports more than 200,000 jobs in university towns and cities across the UK.[60] Total spending by international students and their visitors generates £25.8 billion in gross output in the UK. British colleges and universities have campuses, branches, teaching centres or affiliated institutions stretching from Japan and China to the Middle East, mainland Europe and North America, generating £10.8 billion of UK export earnings. Some private schools are also big foreign currency earners for themselves and their local areas. This money makes British education better and in some cases the best in the world. It also boosts the economy of towns and cities like Aberystwyth, Birmingham, Brighton, Bristol, Canterbury, Exeter, Glasgow, London, Loughborough, Norwich, Manchester, Newcastle, Leeds, St Andrews, Stirling, York, and many others.

Brexit, as we will now see, endangers all these benefits and more. Britain's diverse and inventive education establishments will need to become even more agile to survive Brexit.

Who Teaches Our Children?

Membership of the EU has allowed teachers and other professionals to come to the UK, work and generally have their professional qualifications recognised. The same is true for British teachers going abroad, most obviously to teach English. The 'knowledge economy' has always depended on freedom of movement not just in a technical sense inside the EU but in a more general sense all around the world. And it has been very helpful.

State schools are often short of teachers in specialist subjects and rely on foreign teachers to make up for an under-supply of trained UK citizens. Maths and physics teachers are a particular problem. They are extremely difficult to find and almost impossible to retain. In England, half dropped out within five years of starting their careers, according to the Education Policy Institute think tank. Under half (47%) of GCSE maths teachers in England held a maths or relevant science degree. In disadvantaged areas outside London only 40% had a relevant degree, and in physics, just 17% had a physics degree.

Without teachers from the EU these shortages would have been much starker. We can see this from the number of foreign teachers arriving every year. In order to teach in state schools under local authority control and in special education schools in England and Wales, a foreign teacher must be awarded Qualified Teacher Status. (Scotland and Northern Ireland run similar schemes.) After having their credentials checked, 3,525 people from other EU member states received qualified teacher status in 2017-18. There are about 450,000 full-time equivalent teachers in England. So just one year's batch of foreign teachers made up almost 1% of the workforce, and the total must be much higher.

However the intake of EU teachers in 2017-18 was 25% down on the previous year, including a 33% drop from Poland (where there has been bad publicity about racially-motivated attacks) and a 17% drop in applicants from Spain. Teacher applications from Canada, Australia and New Zealand also fell significantly.

Some 85% of modern foreign language assistants – Marisol's entry level job to teaching in the UK – and 30% of modern foreign language teachers are European nationals.

Ian Hartwright, senior policy adviser at the National Association of Head Teachers, said they would be hard to replace[61]:

'There is no evidence to suggest they [EU teachers] are displacing UK teachers – in fact, they were probably filling gaps and mitigating a recruitment and retention crisis in teaching here and positively improving the lives of young people in England and the UK.'

Writing in the *TES* (formerly the *Times Educational Supplement*), Geoff Barton, general secretary of the Association of School and College Leaders, said of teacher shortages in schools in England and Wales[62]:

'What is notable is that, first, there are a lot of them and, second, the numbers are rising, presumably as a result of the difficulties in home-grown teacher supply where the Department for Education has missed its own recruitment targets in every one of the past five years... And this will put more pressure on the provision of modern foreign language teaching.

'The last thing that we need in subjects where it is already often difficult to recruit — and where take-up at GCSE and A-level is in decline — is another obstacle.'

Scotland, England and Wales

In Scotland, most pupils sit 'Highers' and 'Advanced Highers' instead of A-Levels. University undergraduate honours courses last four years rather than the three they typically do in England. Respected educationalists in Scotland believe Brexit will bring a number of problems. But, again, the issue of teacher shortages is key.

Since the Brexit vote, the General Teaching Council for Scotland says applications from EU qualified teachers to come to Scotland have fallen significantly. Just a handful — a mere 14 EU teachers — applied for registration in Scotland in the year to June 2018. For comparison in previous years applications were at least ten times higher — 159 in 2016 and 186 in 2017.

John Edward, director of the Scottish Council of Independent Schools, complained:[63]

'There were 722 French teachers last year in the state sector, compared with 1,070 in 2008. Over the same period, the number of German teachers has almost halved, to 100.'

He said such shortages were putting at risk the Scottish government's 'admirable ambitions' to improve language skills.

Recognising EU Teaching Qualifications

The government hopes that teachers from the EU will continue to educate British children. Under the proposed Brexit Transition Arrangements, recognition of EU and EEA teaching and other qualifications will continue until December 2020. If all goes to plan, we will then have an 'ambitious agreement' on the mutual recognition of professional qualifications. If it doesn't, Britain could still recognise the qualifications of EU-trained teachers, but the reverse might not be true: British teachers might not be able to work abroad in the EU.

If fewer EU teachers want to travel to the UK after Brexit, some vacancies may be filled by extra new British teachers, or by more qualified teachers from outside Europe, though if that were easy there probably wouldn't be a shortfall in the first place.

In general, leaving the European Union is expected to worsen the problems in British schools. Steve Besley, head of policy at exam board Pearson, said Brexit would be one of the 'top challenges' for schools in the next few years, hitting recruitment, funding and costs. Mr Besley told the National Association of Secondary Moderns' annual conference in 2017 that some EU teachers would inevitably return to their home country, and new recruits would be harder to find.

Some £3 billion of European Structural Funding (ESF) which helps pay for local projects with young people, libraries and adult learning, was also coming to an end. Mr Besley noted that with the UK government under significant post-Brexit pressure to replace EU funding in many other areas, Britain was 'unlikely' to 'plug that hole.' This funding gap comes at a particularly bad time because schools face big rises in other costs, partly as a result of post-referendum currency fluctuations. Following the vote to leave, Microsoft announced a 22% rise in the price of its software services and Apple hiked its computer and laptop prices by about 20% because of a slide in the value of the pound.

Why should we care? Put simply, because we care for the future of our country and the future for our families. Some parents care so much about education they are prepared to sell up and move house to be near a 'good' school.

For decades Britain has attracted many of the best and brightest from around the world to teach here in schools and universities. That pull to the UK is weakening. Moreover, if British children learn fewer languages they will have fewer life and economic opportunities, their world view will become smaller. They may travel less, their horizons shrink, and they become less competitive in the jobs market. Global Britain – if it means anything – means a wider world outlook. It is true that the internal language of many international companies is English, even those with a German or Dutch or French history. But as the chief executive of one Anglo-European conglomerate put it to me: 'Fluency in English is taken for granted. Fluency in at least one other European language, preferably German or French, is necessary to get to the top.'

Even so, Brexit, as always, provides some upside as well as difficulties.

Global Britain – Schools Abroad

English private schools are exploring expansion in mainland Europe, because UK companies and others including American corporations with British staff are relocating to the EU. Dulwich College in London and Wellington College in Berkshire are among those who see a post-Brexit opportunity in providing A-Levels and British educational and cultural standards on the Continent.[64] Amsterdam and Frankfurt are in vogue because UK firms are thinking of relocating there. King's Group, a Madrid-based operator of British international schools in the UK, Spain, Latvia and Panama, has opened a new branch in Frankfurt with 50 students, while the British School of Amsterdam aims to move into a larger campus in 2020 and expand by 20%. All these opportunities are no doubt wonderful for the schools and pupils involved, and the parents or employers who pay for the privilege of a first-class English education. But they are not available to the school at the end of the road, or on the edge of the housing estate.

Day Trips and Visits

Compared to the bigger problems with our children's education, school trips abroad and exchange visits may seem a minor issue. But in 2018 an open letter signed by the British Council, the Association of School and College Leaders, the NAHT headteachers' union and the National Education Union pointed out that 'Britain's future prosperity and place in the world depends on a new generation of outward looking, multilingual, globally minded young people who are prepared to live, work and thrive in the global economy.'[65]

The same is true in reverse. It is clearly important for Britain's 'open' image to encourage foreign students to study here, including those who may spend a few days in London or Edinburgh or elsewhere on a school trip, to get a flavour of our country. The open letter touched on something which may not be top of the government's to-do list, but which nevertheless affects many children and their ambitions for the future. Much of Britain's success in the world has depended on one thing: brain power, and exchanging ideas and theories with other people, including the world's finest minds. It might start with a school trip, or an engaging Spanish teacher who opens a child's eyes to a new culture and a new language. But it may end with ground-breaking research, new ideas, better products, and burnishing of Britain's image as the home of inventive people with eccentric ideas which can sometimes change the world.

Universities, Soft Power and Brexit

The post-Brexit problems with schools are minor compared with those experienced already or anticipated for students and academics in higher education. Universities fear serious problems from losing some of the best brains in the world, otherwise known as their EU staff. They are already experiencing difficulties attracting well-qualified replacements and there are real concerns about loss of research cooperation and funding or co-funding from European institutions.

Spanish universities, to take one example, are planning to close Erasmus scholarships for British students as a result of Brexit. Erasmus is a wonderful programme. It helps students find international study placements and obtain the scholarships which help pay for them. Since Britain is a higher education powerhouse, British students have been among its greatest beneficiaries. The UK remains a member of Erasmus until EU negotiations are complete. What happens beyond 2020, however, is still not clear.

UK participation in the EU's Horizon 2020 programme (more later) has dropped after failures to win grants. Those involved believe these failures are directly linked to Brexit. An academic in London responsible for coordinating applications for various EU funds and joint projects with universities across Europe told me that such cooperation had become increasingly difficult and at times impossible during the Brexit negotiations in 2018. One prestigious northern European university which this academic deals with told her, apologetically, that she was wasting her time because including British institutions in applications for EU grants would fail or be tied up in bureaucratic uncertainty because of Brexit. The academic said that the number of lost opportunities was impossible to quantify because: 'I don't know what we are missing.'

Why Universities Help Those Who Do Not Go There

We do not all go to university. It's a privilege, not a right. And as Michael Gove argued, the British people may 'have had enough of experts.' But we do need qualified and knowlededgable individuals. Mr Gove presumably doesn't get his teeth fixed by some bloke in the pub, or an illness treated by someone he meets in the street.

The Gove children, I assume, are not educated by passing graduates of the University of Life. Nor was the Gove family car constructed by three blokes with screwdrivers hanging around a scrapyard but through the efforts of skilled workers and engineers with university degrees.

More and more of us want to study full time at the 380 accredited universities and colleges across the UK. Currently the Universities and Colleges Admission Service accepts some 700,000 applications a year – around 27% of 18-year-olds. On top of this, there were around 135,000 EU students at UK colleges and universities in 2018.

A report of the government's independent Migration Advisory Committee on the impact of international students in Britain warned that 'the UK leaving the EU poses additional challenges' to students in higher and further education, and in independent and language schools.[66] It stated even more gloomily:

> 'We do not… see any upside for the sector in leaving the EU: any barriers to student mobility are likely to have a negative impact.'

No upside for students. No upside for universities. And no upside either for the towns and cities where educational establishments have such a big economic impact.

Money Matters

UK students (and EU students) at English universities currently are required to pay fees up to £9,250 per year. Tuition fees for non-EU students start at around £10,000 and can top £38,000 for medical degrees. In the most simple cash terms, 135,000 EU students enrich British universities considerably, and they enrich university towns through increased employment opportunities. But this enrichment is not just money. It is also an enrichment of our culture. Students mix, make friends and sometimes fall in love with people from different cultures, with different perspectives and different ideas. This is a petri-dish of creativity, and Brexit puts it at risk.

Fearing a post-Brexit dip in EU student applications, university vice chancellors asked the British government for 'urgent clarification' on the future status of students. It is much needed. The UK Council for International Student Affairs, which assists foreign students who plan to come to the UK, is tasked with making things as easy as possible for these revenue-generating, culture-enriching European students. Instead, UKCISA details the contorted situation for EU students wishing to study in the UK[67] (yes, it is mind-numbingly tedious and that is why I have included it here. If you don't need to know it, you can skip it):

'If a final (Brexit) agreement is reached, EU, non-EU, EEA and Swiss citizens and their eligible family members already in the UK before 30 March 2019 and those who come to the UK during the transitional/implementation period can apply for immigration permission in the UK under a scheme designed by the UK government known as the EU Settlement Scheme. They will need to do this if they wish to remain in the UK after the end of the transitional/implementation period, or otherwise apply under another category of the immigration rules.

'If an agreement between the UK and the EU is not reached, the settlement scheme will operate in much more restricted capacity, and there will be separate provisions for those coming to the UK from 30 March 2019.'

It adds (you can pick up here after the jumble above):

'There has, as yet been no decision on either fee status or student support for those planning to arrive in the UK to study a further or higher education course in the academic year 2020-21.'

And for the following year:

'There have been no decisions on fee status or student support following the UK's full withdrawal from the EU.'

Academics who deal with EU students have told me that such statements are regarded by many students as off-putting as well as confusing. Again, the issue is uncertainty. Attracting undergraduates to England and Wales means a commitment of three years, to Scotland four years. For PhD students the commitment is generally at least three years and four or five years is not uncommon. So ask yourself this – why would any clever student in Hamburg or Perugia or Paris apply for a UK course lasting several years knowing that nothing is certain about their legal status after the first year?

No decisions. No certainty. Probably far fewer student applications.

Hardest Hit Universities

The 24 universities of the Russell Group, plus other London institutions and some in Scotland, are likely to be most affected by this mess. In 2018, some 11% of the total students at Edinburgh University and almost 10% at University College London[68] were from the EU, a total of 7,600.

Seeking to allay fears, and despite what potential applicants might read in the European newspapers or on the websites of the Universities and Colleges Admission Service and UKCISA, England's Education Secretary Damian Hinds confirmed that EU students starting courses in autumn 2019 will pay the same tuition fees as English students. The Welsh and Scottish governments have made soothing noises too. But in my role as Chancellor of the University of Kent and after conversations with EU staff and students I can confirm from personal experience that such assurances are drops of clarity in a soup of uncertainty. Telling a student that things will be fine next autumn when she needs to plan three years ahead is almost pointless. It is not a survival strategy for Brexit or for education or indeed for the reputation of the United Kingdom. It is simply not good enough.

Surviving the Known Unknowns

This uncertainty has already cost British universities. After years of good times and continuous growth, by the beginning of 2019 UK universities reported significant drops in EU student numbers. The Russell Group revealed the number of EU students starting studies in

2018-19 was down 3% on the previous year. Applications for postgraduate courses dropped even more – 9%.

EU research funding will, it is assumed, inevitably fall too. There are also real concerns – which I share – about European academics in the UK deciding to leave and not being easily replaced. In 2017-18, the last academic year for which figures were available, one in five (18%) of academic staff, 37,255, were citizens of other EU states. At the University of Kent, where I am Chancellor, many of our most valued colleagues are EU citizens. We do not want them to leave. Asking EU academics to commit to coming to Britain amid the Brexit turmoil has been difficult.

Professor Dame Nancy Rothwell, president and vice-chancellor of the University of Manchester, one of many top institutions which have seen a fall in enrolment, called the drop in EU students coming to the UK 'an early warning.' The Higher Education Policy Institute think tank predicted EU student applications could drop by as much as 60% when Britain actually leaves the EU.

Research Funding
The UK government says Britain will remain part of the €70 billion Horizon 2020 programme, which funds scientific research. This science fund has allocated €11.4 billion to the UK in the past five years. It has also made assurances that it will compensate universities for any grants lost from the programme. That may be welcome, but details from Westminster on other Brexit-related matters have been characteristically sketchy, and – to take one example – an additional €1.3 billion of EU funds were expected in the next two years from the European Research Council

and Marie Skłodowska-Curie Actions schemes. Whether these funds will arrive or be lost or be replaced is, like much about Brexit, unclear.

In an open letter, organisations which represent more than 150 higher education providers, including Universities UK and the Russell Group, have called on the British government to make up for any reduction in EU research funding. They said that a no deal Brexit would be 'one of the biggest threats our universities have ever faced,' warning:

'It is no exaggeration to suggest that this would be an academic, cultural and scientific setback from which it would take decades to recover.'

Even the variations known as a 'soft Brexit' are viewed with concern. According to the Department for Education, the total revenue generated directly by having approximately 130,000 EU students studying in the UK is enormous – £2.7 billion a year. As we have seen, the 'knock on' or multiplier effect of this cash in terms of spending off campus including spending by those employed in other jobs that are created and by visiting parents and others is put at £25.8 billion. This is an enormous boost (and potential loss) to the UK economy (and indirectly to everyone, whether or not in education).

But while the quantifiable losses are important – the 'facts' we so lacked during the 2016 Brexit campaign – the unquantifiable losses are even more important. As a senior policy analyst at the Russell Group, Hollie Chandler, put it: 'The drop in postgraduate research courses is especially troubling – these students contribute direct-ly to the UK's research capacity.'[69] They make Britain a healthier, wealthier, richer and brainier place.

Our Survival as a Brainy Island Race

Brexit, then, risks diminishing the soft power and hard cash that British education currently holds. Our universities transmit intelligence and influence. More than a third of Nobel prizewinners who studied in a foreign country came at some time in their lives to a British university. At the last count the UK had some 130 Nobel prizes in subjects ranging from physics and chemistry to literature and the peace prize. Affiliates of just one university, Cambridge, have won more than 100 Nobel prizes. That is far more than all of Japan and China put together.

Many foreign leaders have studied in Britain. They include former US president Bill Clinton, Australia's ex-Prime Minister Malcolm Turnbull, Singapore's Prime Minister Lee Hsien Loong and Sheikh Khalifa bin Zayed Al Nahyan, president of the United Arab Emirates, Pakistan's Benazir Bhutto, and Iran's President Hassan Rouhani, as well as King Harald of Norway and other monarchs and royal family members. Often they return home with affection for British people, customs and culture.

From the discovery of penicillin to the Higgs Boson or the World Wide Web, Brainy Britain attracts top talent from around the globe. Knowledge, expertise and science have no international boundaries; wisdom has real freedom of movement.

And the unpalatable truth is that Brexit itself demonstrates what happens when people without real expertise or knowledge manage a difficult project through slogans and articulate a dream without planning for it in reality.

It puts at risk the very visible chains linking experts and researchers worldwide and especially the links between Britain and Europe. No doubt a post-Brexit Britain will maintain some of these links, and some of the prestige – and money – they bring. But university leaders see decades – centuries – of academic excellence and contact with intellectual and other leaders around the world being put in jeopardy, as well as inestimable damage being done to the UK's reputation as a forward-looking and free-thinking nation by what some perceive as a backward-looking nativism of Spitfires and World War Two rhetoric.

When it comes to education, the best that can be said for Brexit is that it will only result in the loss of a teacher here or there and diminish some subjects such as modern languages, which many British people apparently feel they can do without. At its worst, Brexit will be a cultural and educational disaster which makes the UK intellectually poorer, less inventive, and less competent. Damaging education in schools and universities does not improve Britain's reputation. And it is not good for our children and grandchildren either.

5. BREXIT & TRAVEL

One of the most obvious practical problems with Brexit is that it complicates simple things in our lives that we have taken for granted for over 40 years. One of these is how we travel to the Continent. Increased bureaucracy means that hopping on a plane to Prague, a train to Brussels or a ferry to Le Havre will not be so easy. It's already happened.

French Leave

In March 2019, a few days before the first target date for Britain to leave the EU, French customs personnel took several weeks of industrial action. Their work to rule was a warning about a lack of preparation for Brexit on the French side of the Channel. Boarding a Eurostar train is usually fast and frictionless. The industrial action caused chaos. There were long queues at Gare du Nord and St Pancras, with some passengers waiting six hours to get on a train. There were also very long traffic queues in the roads towards Calais port and travellers were advised to change their plans. The protests on the French side were not simply bloody-mindedness on the part of

Gallic officialdom. French customs staff were making an important practical point.

When Britain leaves the EU, it is not just frictionless trade at risk – so, too, is frictionless tourism. Instead of the 30-second glance at a passport from officials we have become used to when travelling to most EU destinations, old-style checks will come into play. For those British travellers of a certain age who remember having to show passport, return ticket and a reasonable amount of money, this is not an attractive prospect. We may be asked many more questions about our reasons for travel and endure detailed inquiries about what is in our suitcases. That means we will be standing in lines at airports for longer. More significantly there could be visa requirements for EU travel.

Under the current freedom of movement rules, as we saw in *Chapter 1. Brexit & Our Food*, Brits can travel abroad freely to all other EU states. With a Brexit deal, EU citizens and UK nationals would probably continue to travel freely with a passport or identity card until the end of a proposed transition period, say in 2020. When the transition period ends the European Commission has offered visa-free travel for UK nationals coming to the EU for a short stay, as long as the UK offers the same in return. But obtaining visa-free travel will come at a price. We Brits will pay a modest fee for visa-waivers and jump through one of the many new bureaucratic hoops that lie ahead.

The fee will be paid under a new EU scheme, the European and Travel Information and Authorisation System, which is scheduled to come into force in 2021. ETIAS is supposed to help secure Europe's borders, especially against people-smugglers and terrorists.

From 2020 it applies to all non-EU citizens entering the Schengen free-travel zone, allowing multiple trips within a three-year period. After Brexit, Britain would be treated as a 'third country.' That designation means Britain would be considered by the EU to be broadly similar to, say, Cuba or Egypt.

Natasha Berthaud, a spokeswoman for the Commission's President Jean-Claude Juncker, tweeted that visitors from post-Brexit Britain would have to fill out an online form and pay €7 (£6) for a visa waiver, valid for three years:

Natasha Bertaud ✔
@NatashaBertaud
   Follow   ∨

Yes #ETIAS will apply to the #UK as 3rd country post-Brexit - 7 euros for a 3 year pre-travel authorisation. Simple form, like #ESTA to the US, but way cheaper. #Brexit #EUCO

3:15 PM - 13 Dec 2018

So Britons will have to obtain an ETIAS, like an ESTA, the American equivalent. But a quick weekend trip to Paris, Rome or Prague is not quite the same as trans-Atlantic travel. And as we have noted, there are some British citizens who live in south-east England who can currently nip across the Channel to Paris for lunch with a minimum of bureaucratic fuss. All that will become more tiresome, though (with a degree of goodwill) still feasible.

Britain's hoteliers, restaurateurs, and tour guides will be hoping the arrangements work well. In 2017, a record number of visitors came to the UK, most from the EU. Europeans flock to the UK every year for their holidays or short breaks, from Italian motorcyclists who enjoy the freedom of single-track roads in the Scottish highlands, to cultural tourists in Bath and York, Dubliners who fancy a weekend in Belfast, or the coach loads of Germans who love the Cornish coast. New bureaucratic procedures could damage the UK's tourist industry, projected to be worth £257 billion by 2025.

British Brexit Bonus

Theresa May's government promised British people a return to the old-style blue passports. Under existing EU rules, Britain could have chosen any colour for our passports anyway. There is no EU regulation telling member states they have to be burgundy (the Croatian passport is blue). More importantly, the Home Office has warned UK travellers must now have at least three months remaining on passports for travel to the European Union – and should renew an expiring passport soon 'to avoid any delay, as the passport issuing service can get busy.'

After Brexit when entering passport control for popular locations like Benidorm, Palma, the Algarve, Paris or the Greek islands, the British will no longer stand in the EU/EEA line. We will join the queue with Chinese, American, Australian, Indian and other third country tourists. Standing in queues is a British tradition, but not one we relish at airports. Perhaps on return to the UK, the British Passports-only lines will be speedier than we are used to. Along with the new blue passports, that may be some compensation for longer queues abroad.

Queuing for Entry

In their work to rule, French border staff were pointing out that France will need more staff once Brexit happens. If the French government does not employ more customs and other officers there is likely to be further and longer lasting significant delays to holidaymakers, business people and lorry and bus drivers. I have friends in the UK Border Force and while some of them criticise their French counterparts for causing inconvenience, they also accept that in terms of recruiting more officers, the French are correct. Britain, they assume, will have to follow suit. The UK Border Force does an exceptional job, but it is constantly under pressure and Brexit increases its problems. In a report in 2018, David Bolt, the UK's chief inspector of borders and immigration, warned that managers felt that staff were so stretched that the Border Force was 'resourced to fail' and our borders were not secure[70]. Staff shortages at key ports – Dover, Portsmouth, Southampton and Poole – meant control of illegal immigration could not be guaranteed. The report bluntly said that officers at Portsmouth:

> 'Told inspectors that migrants were well aware of the Border Force's limited resources, and they would split up and hide in different trailers in the belief that if one was detected the force would not have the capacity to search the other trailers as thoroughly.'

Brexit, therefore, inevitably means either the UK Border Force receives more money so it is 'resourced to succeed' rather than to fail, or queues for ordinary travellers and lorries increase to unacceptable and infuriating levels on both sides of the Channel, and genuine control of our borders against illegal migrants will be impossible.

Backlog at Dover

Brexit threatens to cause big traffic snarl-ups in southern England, particularly in Kent, delaying deliveries, straining the tempers of holidaymakers and lengthening commutes in the crowded south-east.

Some 90% of all freight traffic between the UK and the rest of Europe passes through Dover and the Channel Tunnel entrance at Folkestone a few miles along the coast. Frictionless trade normally means the number of HGV parking spaces at both locations is severely limited. These ports of entry and exit were built on the principle that traffic has to keep flowing. They are therefore vulnerable choke-points for people and goods coming and going to mainland Europe. Severe problems occurred in 2015. There were tailbacks for miles on both sides of the Channel, leading the police to park lorries on the sides of the M20 motorway heading inland from the coast.

Concerns about how Brexit will affect the roads are heightened partly because the Department of Transport has such a poor record. In 2019, it turned Manston airport into a lorry park as part of a trial for Brexit. So few lorries turned up at the airport the local joke was that Chris Grayling, then the Transport Minister, was the only person in Britain unable to organise a traffic jam. If post-Brexit travel goes wrong, it seems fair to say that roads in the south-east could be clogged for some time.

Flying to the Continent

For tourists and business travellers alike, the scariest post-Brexit travel scenario involves preparation for 'no deal.' No deal could bring with it severe problems to travel with predicted massive flight disruption. That's because the UK and airlines licensed in Europe would have had to negotiate new service agreements. Even under a deal with the EU, Brexit could still seriously complicate travel from Britain to destinations outside the EU, although there may be time to avoid the worst problems with lengthy negotiations and legal changes.

The 2007 EU-US Open Skies deal is the key issue. It's a deal between the US and the EU (rather than between the US and Britain) which allows American and European airlines to fly between the US and the EU/EEA and vice-versa. Renegotiating it would be a major headache. That is because the US–EU Open Skies Agreement is a 'mixed agreement' meaning that in some countries like Belgium, national or regional parliaments may need to vote on some of the changes. The Walloon parliament (which delayed an EU-Canada trade deal) could delay any open skies deal involving the UK.

That means after Brexit the deal will have to be rolled over or renegotiated, something which may, or may not, be easily achieved. This is where things get technical. The UK's right to fly to the rest of the European Union and to 17 other countries including the USA is governed by EU law. After Brexit Britain and the EU have agreed to allow 'basic connectivity' for a year. That means passengers are not likely to be stranded. Planes will not be grounded.

Passengers of UK airlines will be able to fly 'point to point,' that's between the UK and another EU country. So a British Airways plane taking off from Glasgow, say, could fly to Madrid. But it does not cover further connecting flights by the same UK carrier between two other EU countries, say, Spain to Germany, without a change in the ownership of the company. To cope with this problem, some airlines have already begun to consider how to change their structure to ensure 'majority' EU ownership. Easyjet has set up a new company in Austria. Ryanair, which is based in Ireland but has many UK shareholders, was confident it would be able to deal with any issues. Likewise, the International Airline Group, which owns BA, Iberia and Aer Lingus, told the BBC[71]:

'We are confident that we will comply with the EU and the UK ownership and control rules, post-Brexit.'

All it takes is time, and lawyers. Reassuringly for passengers, air navigation services will remain under international obligations laid out within the Chicago Convention and the 1944 International Air Services Transit Agreement. Air travel should remain as safe as it is now.

Other Modes of Travel

For those taking coach tours abroad, the government website warned:

'Bus and coach services to non-EU countries, for example Switzerland or Andorra, may not be able to run. The government is working to make sure these continue with minimal or no disruption. Check back for updates or contact the company you booked with if you've any questions.'

Ferries are covered by international agreements which should not be affected.

Holiday Protection

According to a survey for ABTA, the Association of British Travel Agents, which represents travel agents and tour operators, the number of Britons taking a holiday remained high after the referendum. Some 86% of respondents took a holiday at home or abroad in the 12 months to August 2018 (87% in 2017). However, the average number of trips, including 'stay-cations,' holidays in the UK, fell from 3.8 to 3.4 per person. For those worried about post-Brexit travel, there is little advice that can be offered in such an uncertain situation. ABTA recommends booking a package holiday (of the type its members offer) with a UK-based company because it will continue to be covered by Package Travel Regulations, offering a full refund if the holiday cannot be provided.

Health Cards

Many British people – an estimated 27 million of us – have EHICS, the European Health Insurance Card. These cards mean that if we fall ill in the EU (also Switzerland, Norway, Iceland and Lichtenstein) we can expect similar treatment to at home without further private insurance. They cover pre-existing medical conditions, accidents and emergencies. The plan has been for EHICs to remain valid during a negotiated transition period, to the end of 2020. With no deal, EHICS would in theory immediately become invalid, and if the precise nature of the UK leaving the EU is in doubt the advice is for UK travellers to buy health insurance just as if we were travelling outside the EU. There could of course be further emergency measures or short term reciprocal arrangements. ABTA advises checking your private insurance, including for travel disruption.

Mobile Phone Charges

The European Union forced mobile phone operators to cease charging EU customers more for using their phone in another member state. These old 'roaming charges' could return and they can be very expensive.[72] The UK government has capped them by law at £45 a month until the end of 2020. The government advises:

> 'Check with your phone operator to find out about any roaming charges you might get after 31 October 2019. A new law means that you're protected from getting mobile data charges above £45 without you knowing. Once you reach £45, you need to opt in to spend more so that you can continue using the internet while you're abroad. Your phone operator will tell how you can do this.'

Driving Abroad, Buses and Coaches

Before a trip to the EU27 I dropped into my local post office to ask about an International Driving Permit (IDP). At the moment, as millions of British tourists know, a British driving licence is good enough to rent a car in

France, Spain or any other EU/EEA country. But my friendly post office staff advised me to buy an IDP for £5.50 just in case. And there was a catch. I needed two International Driving Permits, because different countries obey different international systems. One is valid for three years for all of the EU except Spain, Malta and Cyprus. The other licence covering those three states, Spain, Malta and Cyprus, is only valid for one year.

The British government advises that if you are taking a car abroad you take your UK driving licence, your V5C log book, a free 'green card' from your car insurance company (which could take a month to obtain), and a GB sticker[73]. British nationals living in the EU have been told to exchange their British licence for an EU one because if there is a no deal Brexit they may have to sit a driving test.

Pet Passports

My Kerry Blue terrier, Wallace, has a Pet Passport and has travelled with us to France and Germany. Frictionless travel for dogs is not entirely possible – he needs various jabs and certificates from our vet, and a further check on the way back, but it is fairly simple. The hope is that this system or something similar will continue after Brexit to avoid the old system which included lengthy periods for animals in quarantine. In the meantime, ask your vet. The government says that in the worst case pet travel could take up to four months to arrange.[74]

6. BREXIT & OUR COUNTRY

A few years ago, inspired by a BBC TV programme which investigated family histories, Strathclyde University did a genealogical search on my own family. The results were mostly quite boring, but they did find that a dozen members of my family signed the Ulster Covenant against Irish Home Rule in 1912. Six signed with a cross, suggesting they were illiterate. The professor in charge of the research traced my family back to Germany in the 12th century in Nuremberg and said that from the 17th century – when the Eslers escaped Germany as refugees from the 30 Years War – one word ran through my family background in Scotland and Ireland: 'Protestant.' I was born into a council house in Clydebank on the outskirts of Glasgow, and shared that house with my mother, father, grandmother, and two aunts. A few years later we moved to Edinburgh and then to Northern Ireland. I have also lived in London, Cardiff, Leeds and Kent.

I recount these otherwise insignificant personal details because when it comes to Brexit it seems that our country itself, at least as it is presently constituted, may not survive. We live in an increasingly dis-United Kingdom, divided by widening political, cultural and societal faultlines which risk pulling apart hundreds of years of efforts to forge Scotland, England, Wales and parts of Ireland into the successful national invention we call 'being British.' In 2016, Scotland and Northern Ireland voted to Remain in the EU while England and Wales voted to Leave.

This has caused acute ill-feeling in Scotland, where many Scots (and not just nationalists) are angry they are being dragged out of a union with Europe which they want because of a union run by a Westminster parliament which they no longer much respect.

But the divisions we now have to recognise and survive as a result of Brexit go much deeper. During the Brexit campaign and subsequently, some of our fellow citizens have denied facts and responded to polite differences of opinion and reasoned argument with abuse. Brexit has brought out some of the worst in us, as well as some of the best.

Social media is a reflection of some of the worst. On Twitter, Facebook and elsewhere the Brexit lexicon (from both pro – and anti – activists) has included terms such as elite, establishment, out of touch, Judas, quisling, traitor, scum, anti-democratic, fake news, snowflake, liar, Tory, toff, racist, stupid, far left, and so on. There are the usual swear words. The imprecation to 'grow a pair' appears surprisingly often, although it's unclear why more testosterone would help an often bull-headed discussion. Some have even raised the bizarre suggestion that anyone dissenting from a full Brexit (whatever that may mean) is in the pay of George Soros, a Jewish billionaire and philanthropist. This is often seen as part of an anti-Semitic trope about 'Jewish conspiracies.'

The insults point out the strength of feeling about Brexit. But also that the 2016 referendum and its aftermath have not increased civility in public discourse. On the contrary, people on the other side are characterised not merely as being wrong, but as wicked. Some politicians and newspaper headlines have made inflammatory speech part of their appeal. In 2016, the *Daily Mail* described judges involved in a controversial Brexit decision as 'Enemies of the People,' a phrase associated with the Nazis and the propaganda of Josef Goebbels. By 2018, the Conservative business minister Richard Harrington described members of the hardline pro-Brexit European Research Group led by Jacob Rees-Mogg as 'traitors' to the Conservative Party. Similar language has been used within the Labour Party's internal feuding.

Such strains and divisions are also known to many of us in our communities and families. I know personally of a British Asian friend who has lived in the UK since childhood in the 1970s who says she has been racially abused more often since 2016 than in the years before. A Chinese friend married to a white Englishman was embarrassed to be shouted at in racial terms in London's Hyde Park, something which had never happened to her anywhere in many years living in the UK. Several friends have told me they cannot discuss the subject with certain members of their family or with neighbours or at the school gate. But beyond the anecdotes, there are also some facts about our divisions and how they may be healed. Or not.

Dis-United Kingdom and the 'Elite'

In the 2016 referendum, beyond the divisions between Scotland, Northern Ireland, England and Wales, the people of England were themselves deeply divided. London voted overwhelmingly Remain. Rural areas such as Cornwall, and old industrial areas in the north east of England often voted Leave. Stoke on Trent was called Britain's Brexit Capital by the erstwhile UKIP leader Paul Nuttall. The Potteries voted 69% to Leave. These divisions have been compared to bitterly contested views over the Iraq war in 2003.

After the 2016 vote a Twitter meme showed the London Underground Northern Line stations – Camden Town, Kentish Town, Tufnell Park, (all strong Remain areas) then a dotted line through all of the rest of England (which was empty space) until the rail link resurfaced in Edinburgh, also overwhelmingly Remain. The joke was clear – but so was the notion that a vast swathe of England could be ignored, at least by the artist.

On the Brexit side, the multi-millionaire Brexit funder Arron Banks was among those who railed against an anti-Brexit 'establishment' and 'elite', who, he claimed, were destroying what was otherwise a marvellous idea championed by him and his friends (in the title of his book) *The Bad Boys of Brexit*. The campaign tried and often succeeded in re-defining the word 'elite' to mean anyone you don't like or who disagrees with you. In 2019 the former UKIP leader Nigel Farage took the same tack when he launched his new Brexit Party, claiming 'the establishment' was preventing a 'proper' Brexit from happening. Mr Farage went to a fee-paying school, worked in the City of London like his father, had been an Member of the European Parliament for 20 years and his party was backed by very rich donors. As he took on 'the establishment' he announced one of his party's candidates for the 2019 European elections, Annunziata Rees-Mogg, Jacob's sister. Both in rhetoric and in reality the divisions caused by Brexit could not have been clearer.

In his book *Social Class in the 21st Century*, Mike Savage, a professor at the London School of Economics, argued that the idea of three British classes – working class, middle class, and upper class – was out of date. He divided Britain into seven categories, and at the top was the 'elite.' Professor Savage defined this elite as the wealthiest and most privileged group, people who went to private school, Oxford and Cambridge Universities, and who enjoy high cultural activities such as classical music and opera. This 'elite' definition is precisely the group which includes leading Brexit supporters such as Old Etonians Boris Johnson and Jacob Rees-Mogg, hedge fund specialists and multi-millionaires such as Lord Ashcroft, Lord Pearson, James Dyson and the richest man in Britain, Sir James Ratcliffe. With some semantic ju-jitsu, Arron Banks – the multi-millionaire – and others managed, at least in the minds of some in the British public, to turn the definition of the loathed elite from Eton, Oxford and millionaires on its head. 'Elite' in the Brexit aftermath has become, at least in some circles, a description of all those Brexit sceptics who happen to be economists, scientists, historians, university professors, the 'media elite' and other so-called 'intellectuals' plus the

World Economic Forum, the IMF, the World Bank, and many business groups and researchers.

The 'elite' and 'the establishment' have therefore become less terms which describe a social class or group, and rather signifiers of the profound divisions among us. This was further exacerbated by those anti-Brexit activists who insist that the level of education among those who voted for Brexit tends not to include a university education, whereas university educated voters tended to vote Remain. The implication – and sometimes the clear statement – was that Leave voters were stupid. Talking about people you disagree with as elites or as stupid, has hardly helped bring us together.

What follows then is an examination of three areas where Brexit has affected the social fabric of the UK:

- First, relations between races and classes amid allegations of increased 'hate crime.'

- Second, the future of the United Kingdom, especially Scotland and Northern Ireland, places in which large numbers of the population wish to leave the UK.

- Third, the possibilities for a supposed 'Global Britain' or alternatively a 'Little England' vision of the future.

If our country – a United Kingdom of four separate nations with different cultures and many different races – is to survive after Brexit then we need to come to terms and fix our disunity. That means toning down the rhetoric and facing up to the existing problems to prevent them becoming worse in future. Remaining a tolerant country cannot be taken for granted. Remaining a United Kingdom certainly cannot be taken for granted when breaking away from the EU. In Northern Ireland Sinn Fein has already called for a new border poll in the hope of bringing about Irish unity. In Scotland, the SNP government has been more cautious, but SNP activists hope the problems caused by Brexit will finally give them a majority in favour of independence. And in England, both Labour and the Conservative parties have shown themselves to be disunited over Brexit, with some MPs from both splitting away to form the new party, ChangeUK, and other MPs being prepared to defy and vote against their party leadership in different ways. The evidence of disunity therefore stretches from divisions within the Cabinet and Shadow Cabinet right down to hate crimes and far-right protests, which sometimes turn violent.

Did Hate Crime Rise After the Referendum?

The short answer to the question of whether the incidence of hate crimes rose after the 2016 referendum is: 'Yes, it did.' But as with industries or corporations pulling out of the UK, it is often difficult to say with absolute certainty that a particular hate crime was directly related to Brexit or sparked by another factor, or several factors taken together. To repeat the scientific wisdom, correlation does not mean causation. Nevertheless, the evidence on hate crimes goes far beyond anecdotes to statistics collected by the police, by Muslim, Jewish and other groups, and by the United Nations. One Brexit-related hate crime immediately stands out.

On 16 June 2016, a week before the referendum, Jo Cox, the British Labour MP for Batley and Spen was shot and stabbed to death. It was the first killing of a sitting British MP since the Conservative Ian Gow was murdered by the IRA in 1990. When asked to give his name in court Cox's murderer, Thomas Mair, replied 'my name is death to traitors, freedom for Britain.' Witnesses said at the time of the killing Mair shouted out 'This is for Britain,' 'Keep Britain independent', and 'Put Britain first.' Batley and Spen voted 55% to Leave. Mair, who had a history of mental health problems, was found guilty of murder and sentenced to life, with the intent that he should never be released, a 'whole life' order.

How Others See Us and Xenophobia

In the aftermath of the Brexit vote, what has been striking is how little coverage in the British media has been given to the ways in which other countries or non-UK organisations see developments here. Much of the coverage in the UK has suggested that foreign countries, especially in the EU, are obsessed with events in Britain and some claim that they are 'blocking Brexit.'

The truth is that Brexit news in many other countries is far from mainstream, and the fascination often has comic intent. Brexit, and the eccentricities of the British including the parliamentary system and the Speaker John Bercow bellowing at MPs has featured in comedy programmes from the US to the EU, and as far away as South Africa, Australia and New Zealand. But the intricacies of Brexit remain far from the agenda for newspapers or politicians anywhere outside Britain, except perhaps in Ireland.

In Germany, foreign news often begins with Trump or Turkey, Russia, Poland and Hungary, relations with Macron, perhaps Spain and Catalonia, some coverage of the political problems in Italy. Britain, Brexit and the eccentricities of Jacob Rees-Mogg may be in the mix, but Brexit is certainly not prominently on the political agenda. More interesting is to see how others, including the UN, evaluate our peculiar circumstances, our dis-unity and division.

The UN Report

In 2018 the UN Committee on the Elimination of Racial Discrimination sent a 'special rapporteur' to the UK to examine claims of racism and xenophobia in the UK after Brexit. Tendayi Achiume, professor of law at UCLA, reported[75] that some hate crimes were directly connected to the heated Brexit rhetoric that we have experienced, and she pointed the finger directly at political leaders.

'British politicians,' she said, 'helped fuel a steep rise in racist hate crimes during and after the EU referendum campaign.' It's worth reading some of her report at length:

'58. In the days following the EU referendum, the government reported a spike in the number of hate crimes in England and Wales, recording 80,393 offences for the period 2016-2017. This figure represents a 29% increase from the previous year and the highest increase in proportion since 2011. Home Office data on hate crimes showed that in the aftermath of the Brexit vote, 78% of recorded hate crimes were racially motivated and 7% religiously motivated.

'59. It is also important to draw attention to the increase in anti-Semitic hate speech and violence that accompanied and followed the referendum. In 2017, anti-Semitic incidents reached a record level in the UK, with 1,382 anti-Semitic incidents recorded nationwide by the Community Security Trust. This figure represents a 3% increase compared to 2016, and was the highest annual total that the organisation recorded since it began gathering such data in 1984. The number of violent anti-Semitic assaults increased by 34% compared to the previous year. The data showed that 50% of incidents were attributed to the far right.

'62. Another Brexit-related trend that threatens racial equality in the UK has been the growth in the acceptability of explicit racial, ethnic, and religious intolerance, in ways that that the different stakeholders I consulted believed marked a notable shift. On the one hand, for example, extreme right-wing parties have not enjoyed political success in the UK in ways analogous to other parts of Europe. But on the other hand, various stakeholders raised the concern that extreme views—on both the right and left ends of the political spectrum—have gained ground in mainstream political parties in parliaments across the UK.

Newspapers would take these findings seriously were they about an important foreign country, but such reports were ignored or dismissed by much of the British press. (One of our biggest papers, the *Daily Mail,* has itself been accused of xenophobia and its critics on social media often display a montage of front pages which in their view stir up anti-migrant feeling). *The Spectator* magazine simply suggested the hate crime and Brexit issue was all a matter of some doubt[76]:

'Perhaps the referendum did lead to a rise in hate crime. Then again, perhaps it didn't. But despite the angry reports blaming Brexit, the only thing that is clear is that there is little proof either way.'

That may be how right of centre journalists evaluate the evidence but it is not how it is viewed by independent academic researchers.

Research on Hate Crime & Brexit

Police in England and Wales recorded almost 36,000 hate crimes in 2011-12, and roughly twice that number, 71,000 by 2017-18. The Home Office said the increase was driven by improvements in the way police record hate crime but also by 'spikes in hate crime following certain events such as the EU referendum and the terrorist attacks in 2017.'

Daniel Devine, a PhD researcher at the University of Southampton, showed 'the [2016] referendum increased hate crimes by 31 a day, or 638 in a month, depending which data is used.'[77] Devine concluded:

'The evidence strongly supports the conclusion that the referendum led to an increase in hate crimes – potentially even more than the terrorist attacks in Manchester and London did. But why?...A plausible answer lies in the negative framing and focus of immigrants during the campaign, which came to a head during the referendum.'

The UN, the Home Office and academic research appear to agree that Brexit sparked a rise in hate crimes.

The Will of the (Scottish) People

I was in Scotland on the day when it voted No to independence in 2014 by 55%-45% and reported on the result for the BBC. I was also in Scotland for the EU referendum two years later when it voted by a much larger margin to stay in Europe (62% Remain) and in the capital, Edinburgh, (75% Remain). Remarkably, every one of Scotland's 32 electoral regions voted to Remain in the EU. On both occasions many Scots felt that their concerns were largely ignored by the Westminster government.

Perhaps the views of five million Scots are not particularly interesting to 59 million fellow citizens in England and Wales (though people in Northern Ireland have always been culturally closer and more interested in Scottish affairs.) But, make no mistake, the views of the Scottish people could change life in the UK fundamentally.

If Scotland is taken out of the EU 'against its will', Scotland's First Minister Nicola Sturgeon wants to hold another referendum on independence by 2021. She argues that Brexit is bad for Scotland, bad for the UK, bad for Europe and any version of it will make Scots poorer without any significant benefits. SNP activists see Brexit, although unwelcome, as a major boost to the chances of securing their cherished ultimate goal of independence. They may be correct. But there is a significant problem. Brexit may make a second independence vote more likely, if not inevitable. But it does not necessarily make it more likely that Ms Sturgeon and the SNP will actually win it. While the Labour and Conservative parties are relatively weak north of the border, many Scots remain small-c 'conservatives' who are alarmed at the prospect of such a sudden change in their country. Having witnessed what many see as the Brexitshambles of the UK destroying a union with Europe which has lasted less than 50 years, they will need to be convinced that ending a Union of Parliaments begun in 1707 is worth the trouble. Money is also at stake.

Official figures show that Scotland's biggest trading partner is the rest of UK. Will Scots swap a British single market for a newly active border with their biggest customers in England? And will Scots be content to lose money under the 'Barnett formula' and other agreements by which Scotland benefits from being in the United Kingdom by around £15 billion every year?

Sentiment and loathing of Westminster and ridicule of some English Tory politicians often pulls the hearts of Scots in one direction. But economics – the original Scottish 'dismal science', the phrase coined by the Scottish writer Thomas Carlyle and pioneered by Kirkcaldy's Adam Smith – may tug in another.

So far the polls have not yet shown any dramatic surge towards independence. It is not an easy sell and the balance is still roughly 50-50. But younger Scots are more likely to support independence, and Brexit may well pull Scotland further apart from England when other problems start to come to the surface.

Speculation: An Independence Scenario

It's fair to say most Scots – for or against – have thought about independence for years. The rest of the UK, with a few blips, has not paid much attention to it. So, if there is a second independence referendum (likely in my view) and if the SNP were to win this time round (possible, but by no means certain), what would happen? Would an independent Scotland be in the EU and accept the euro? The pound? It's own currency? The answers to these questions are unclear, although new accession countries to the EU are expected to accept the euro. However, this can be accepted in principle and yet delayed in practice. Sweden accepted the euro in 1993, but for Swedes the conditions to switch from the Swedish kroner are yet to be met. No one in the EU pushes Sweden on this. They will not push Scotland either.

Would there be a new EU border between Glasgow and Carlisle? In theory, yes. But both Scotland and England would want a 'soft' border with minimal checks and if possible no interference to trade. (Think Northern Ireland and the Irish Republic.) *Export Statistics Scotland*, a compendium of the Scottish government's own figures, shows that in 2016 Scotland exported more than £45 billion in goods and services to England, Wales and Northern Ireland. Exports to the EU were £12.7 billion. Scots living in the rest of the UK, and rest of the UK citizens living in Scotland would undoubtedly have the right to remain as now. Scotland, to its credit, has been extremely welcoming to new arrivals. Migrants – including those of English origin – are cherished by the Scottish government.

But other changes might cause problems. The SNP is committed to getting rid of nuclear weapons. If England and Wales want Trident or its successors to survive, they would have to find a new home for such a controversial system, at an estimated cost of at least £20 billion.[78]

Moreover, with the US, China, Russia and France, the United Kingdom is a permanent member on the Security Council of the United Nations. Would the 'Rest of the UK' retain its position as one of the Permanent Five – including the power of veto? The European Union as an entity, Japan, India and Brazil all have their eye on 'P5' status. When I discussed this possibility with a serving British ambassador, he replied: 'If we are threatened with losing our veto power at the UN, then we will veto it.' It was a Foreign Office joke, but it could well be true: Britain's UN Security Council veto might survive even if the UK were to fall apart.

Of course, none of these scenarios may come to pass. But what has happened already is a degree of dismay and sourness that after the 2014 independence referendum, the destiny of the Scots is once more in the hands of the English. As one SNP MP at Westminster put it to me: 'Scotland has less clout at Westminster than a group of far right Tories led by Jacob Rees-Mogg.'

The Will of the People (of Northern Ireland)

While my family roots are both in Glasgow and in County Antrim, among the largely Protestant and Unionist communities, sometimes called the 'Scots-Irish,' some relatives live in the Irish Republic. Travelling across Ireland from North to South it's obvious that the Irish Republic has undergone deep economic cultural and social changes since joining the EU along with Britain in the 1970s. Ireland is now richer, more diverse, more outward looking, and less in thrall (as many of my fellow Protestants in Northern Ireland would see it) to the most conservative elements of Irish Catholicism. Referendums have liberalised divorce and legalised gay marriage and abortion.

Ireland is also now more likely to look east to the EU rather than, as was traditionally the case, west to the United States. EU membership helped create 'a Celtic Tiger,' even though that boom was followed by bust in 2008. Ireland has now recovered well.

Northern Ireland has changed radically, too. It was rebuilt after the Troubles and the vast majority of people in both the nationalist and unionist communities remain, as they always were, decent, friendly, hard working, hospitable, and law-abiding. The genius of EU membership has been that both Irish nationalists and British unionists can see the Irish border as an opportunity rather than a problem. It survives on a map, and in theory, but not in practical day to day life. It is Schrödinger's border. It is there for those who need it, not there for those who don't.

Northern Ireland or the border were not significant issues in England, Scotland or Wales during the 2016 Brexit campaign. But the border has most certainly been a sticking point in the Brexit negotiations, although the reason is sometimes misunderstood. The Irish border in the Brexit negotiations is not the border between Ireland and the United Kingdom. It is the border between the European Union's 27 remaining states and the country which wishes to leave. Ireland, with a population of just 4.8 million has not thwarted the grand designs of the United Kingdom of 66 million. The European Union of almost 500 million members is standing up for all its members over the Irish border. The border, in other words, is seen as a great test of EU solidarity which, from the Brussels perspective, the EU has passed.

The good news – for Northern Ireland at least – is that the UK-EU agreement and the proposed transitional arrangements mean Northern Ireland may turn out to be the one area of the United Kingdom least affected by Brexit. In many respects it will survive with no or little change to the cow pastures of County Down, the creameries in County Antrim or Fermanagh, or the creative industries thriving in Belfast, the home of *Game of Thrones*. What then follows is either very good news or very bad news depending on your political leanings.

A border poll – a referendum – was held in Northern Ireland in 1973 and nationalists (mostly Catholics) boycotted it, knowing they would lose. They did. Almost 100% of the votes went to remaining in the UK. The poll was a charade, however, delivering the kind of result that we expected from Cold War communist regimes in eastern Europe. Neither the government of the Irish Republic nor that in Westminster wants another border poll. Moreover the people of Northern Ireland mostly do want a close relationship with the Irish Republic. As with Scotland, another poll may eventually happen, although probably in the long term. Schrödinger's border seems the best and most likely solution, with the Irish border surviving Brexit in good health – existing on a map and in law, but not for most people in reality.

Yet the Brexit debate furthered one serious point of division – the notion that UK politicians haven't a clue about Ireland. One Conservative former government minister, Priti Patel MP, suggested using food shortages to force Ireland to come to a better deal. Since the 1840s Great Famine has been the most emotive issue in Irish political life, Ms Patel's contribution was seen as spectacularly dim-witted and offensive across all of Ireland. Boris Johnson suggested the Irish border was a bit like the border between Islington and Westminster. (It isn't.) The Northern Ireland Secretary Karen Brady admitted she did not know people in Northern Ireland voted on sectarian lines. And Dominic Raab, while Brexit Secretary, could not find the half hour necessary to read the 35 pages of the Good Friday Agreement, the most important Anglo-Irish document since partition in the 1920s.

Moving to Ireland

One other fact about Ireland may prove significant. By October 2018, the Ireland Department of Foreign Affairs reported 158,763 applications for Irish passports from UK citizens in the previous 10 months. This was more than double the 'normal' rate of applications. An Irish passport is effectively an EU passport. After Brexit, more British people want to be Irish.

Disunited Kingdom

For the United Kingdom to survive Brexit, if it means anything, it means finding some way to resolve the differences in our country preferably amicably and at the very least without violence. Re-uniting the United Kingdom will not be easy. But the most important point to remember is that Brexit did not create divisions over the border in Northern Ireland, between Scotland and England, racial hatred and other hate crimes. But it has exacerbated them. Worse, the inflammatory words and actions of some in political life, have – as psychologists would put it – 'given permission' for some of the most violent and racially motivated people in our society to push the boundaries of what is acceptable speech, to threaten others with violence, and to engage in hate crimes. This will take years to put right, if that is even possible.

7. A NO DEAL BREXIT

One of the more revealing media exchanges during the 2019 European Parliament election campaign took place on BBC Radio. Lucy Harris, a Brexit Party candidate claimed voters wanted their 'sovereignty' back 'at any cost.' When asked what cost she personally could stomach she replied that 'in the short term there will be an effect.' She defined those setbacks as lasting 'the next 30 years.' Lucy Harris may well be correct in assuming decades of dislocation and slower growth.

So far in this book we have looked at the best-case predictable Brexit scenario – that is, leaving in an orderly fashion, with transitional arrangements during which the UK can negotiate trade and other deals with the EU and elsewhere to mutual benefit. But since the Brexit Party leader Nigel Farage and others have hardened towards a 'no deal' Brexit and trading on 'WTO rules,' the consequences of these drastic scenarios need to be considered. If, as almost all leading economists argue, any Brexit makes Britain poorer, 'no deal' is particularly brutal.

What No Deal Means

No deal means Britain immediately ceases to be an EU member state. The 585-page Withdrawal Agreement would not apply. There would be no transition period. Britain would crash out without having renegotiated our complex relationship with the EU and, through the EU, with other countries. There would be considerable ill-will. Governments across the EU 27 would see the UK as a 'wrecker.'

The entire legal basis of UK trade with the EU would change. According to economists, leaving Europe's trading bloc to trade on World Trade Organisation (WTO) rules would be like quitting the Premier League to play non-league football. A paper by the UK Institute for Government outlines some of the consequences thus:

- The UK becomes a third country, with no preferential deal for customs purposes or for VAT

- Licenses and approvals issued by the UK are no longer recognised by the EU

- Companies based in the UK can no longer operate in the EU as a member state and need to either move business or establish a representative in an EU country

- The UK is no longer an approved destination for some EU business (eg. ship recycling, some waste management)

- UK professional qualifications are not recognised by the EU

- The UK stops being part of EU systems – like aviation or energy

It goes on. British medical, nursing, teaching, accountancy and other qualifications would no longer be recognised by EU countries.

For businesses there would be a new tariff regime and new customs and regulatory checks. Any British exporter would be required to fill in new documents and paperwork to send goods to any EU country. Businesses would have to prove products complied with EU rules of origin, customs duties and VAT. Nowadays that compliance is simply assumed.

A lorry driver would need different certification and licences. Livestock and food products being exported from the UK into the EU would be subject to new checks since Britain would be deemed no longer compliant with EU rules and standards. This would lead to extended delays at Channel ports, plus higher costs for food, cars, clothing, medicines, other goods exported to the EU plus more bureaucracy, more time in traffic queues, and more tailbacks at Dover.

As mentioned in *Chapter 5. Brexit & Travel*, the UK would no longer be covered by the US-EU Open Skies Agreement.

Ardent Brexiters argue no deal would 'save' the UK the £39 billion 'divorce bill' and other charges. More likely the EU, or any member state of the 27, could hold up progress on any Open Skies or other agreement until Britain stumps up the cash. Moreover, failure to pay bills seriously damages a country's credit rating and reputation. Far from holding all the cards, Britain would be forced to hand over the entire pack to Brussels.

No Deal in Detail: Trade, Shopping and Medicines

UK government plans for no deal mean that, as a temporary measure, there would be no tariffs on most goods coming into the UK. Some industries might be protected from being undercut by imports, including meat and dairy producers or car manufacturers. Trade with non-EU countries which have trade deals with the EU would continue, according to the government. But would that really be the case? Might a lorry load of olives or washing machines coming from Turkey still be hit by more paperwork? As we have noted, the UK has failed to 'roll over' key trade agreements, including those between the EU and Turkey or Japan. This is a big problem. If we have a withdrawal agreement, the EU promises to write to all countries which it has an agreement with, such as on trade, aviation, customs or data, to ask them to treat the UK as an EU member state during the transition period. But since no deal means No Transition, that means no breathing space. All bets are off.

Since a third of the UK's food is imported from the EU, higher prices and shortages of some goods are likely, potentially resulting in empty supermarket shelves. Under no deal, the Bank of England forecast a 5-10% rise in food prices. Bureaucratic delays at ports risk food going stale or becoming inedible. With no deal the UK's refrigerated warehouses would fill up with medicines, but that would not solve all the problems for dislocated drug supplies. Price increases would erode the NHS budget. Newspapers would carry harrowing stories of people unable to receive their prescription drugs or diagnoses. An airlift of essential drugs might help affected patients. Of course, there is much conjecture here: it is the best available information. But the stakes are high.

Citizens' Rights

The status of both EU citizens living in the UK and British nationals living in the EU would be undermined. The UK government promises to guarantee the rights of the estimated three million EU citizens in the UK, but the details have yet to be finalised. Parliament's Human Rights Committee warned these EU citizens could be denied access to council housing, social security and other benefits. British citizens in France, Spain and elsewhere may have similar problems. Legally, they will be citizens of 'third countries' and their new host countries may not offer them any advantages over any other migrants. The Northern Ireland border issue will continue to rankle, although clearly it is in no one's interests – except that of Republican paramilitaries – to stoke up difficulties. The Irish government says it will not allow the border to become a 'backdoor' to goods coming into the EU from Northern Ireland, but no one has explained how that can be achieved without border checks of the kind the EU and UK have ruled out. And the big question here is one of whether the environment will feel more hostile. Will EU27 and UK citizens in each other's countries feel secure? Will they leave? No one, not even those involved, can say for sure.

What are WTO Rules?

The World Trade Organisation is the global body governing international trade. It only really affects countries which do not have free trade agreements. Most of the world, and all rich countries, do have free trade agreements. Space does not permit an account of countries which are said to trade 'only' under WTO rules. It's not that simple. Mauritania is often mentioned as the 'only' country which does so. But Mauritania does have some trading agreements.

The default position for the UK-EU relationship in the case of no deal is that WTO rules would apply not just on EU-UK trade but also between the UK and other countries including those with which the EU has trade deals. That means that under WTO rules the UK would have to grant the same 'most favoured nation' market access to all other WTO members. And as we saw in *Chapter 2. Brexit, Our Health & the NHS*, that would mean exports from the UK to the EU would be subject to the same customs checks, tariffs and regulatory barriers that the EU charges on trade with third party countries such as the US.

New tariffs would increase costs for importers, exporters and consumers. Prices would go up. We could have new trade arrangements but these – under WTO rules – have to be 'non-discriminatory' with potentially a big impact on British farmers and producers. The real problem is not tariffs but 'non-tariff barriers' – customs checks, border controls, form filling, regulations and different standards. The service sector – finance, legal, accountancy insurance and other services – makes up 80% of the UK economy. Businesses in the service sector are particularly vulnerable to a no deal Brexit and non-tariff barriers. The Centre for Economic Performance predicts no deal could cut the UK's trade with the EU27 by 40% over ten years, and a drop in UK income per head of 2.6% per year.[79]

Britain After Brexit? Or After No Brexit?

For some readers the facts about Brexit may be of less significance than their feelings about Europe. Not since the period 1938-1940 have we faced such a momentous decision about where we are going, and what kind of country we want to be. It has not been possible to look in detail at every possible scenario for the future. And of course the EU itself is changing. Far right and populist groups hostile to the EU have gained a toehold in Italy and central European states in ways not seen since the 1930s. On the other hand, approval for the EU has risen in many countries, including Ireland, where the stout defence of the Irish government position by the EU27 has been noted with considerable approval.

Predicting the future is difficult. But we can at least try to choose our future. The facts in this book were largely unknown or ignored when we voted to Leave in 2016. Now we have more facts, British voters need the chance to give their informed consent about the future. As to the precise way out of our increasing difficulties over Brexit, that is beyond the scope of this slim volume.

But the principle seems clear. In 1947, an American diplomat George Kennan wrote an influential short article in a foreign affairs magazine on the threat he saw from Stalin and Soviet communism. Kennan's words helped spur Americans and Europeans into action, leading to the formation of NATO and eventually the European Union. To paraphrase Kennan, the Brexit issue, like dealing with the USSR, is a test of the overall worth of the United Kingdom as 'a nation among nations.' To avoid serious dislocation the UK 'need only measure up to its own great traditions and prove worthy of preservation as a great nation.'

Britain has great traditions, and possibly a great future. And Britain is, and has always been, better than Brexit.

JARGON & THE BORING STUFF

One of the reasons Brexit is so tricky is that understanding what it means is often highly technical and – frankly – tedious. Most of us have managed to get along for most of our lives without understanding the jargon which follows. Certainly that has been the case for some MPs who simply do not know what they are talking about. They brandished some of the terms below with great confidence and zero competence. Many did not understand why the Irish border might be a problem. Many failed to comprehend what the World Trade Organisation is and does. Some failed to understand the difference between tariff and non-tariff barriers to trade.

You don't need to know all these technical bits, but knowing a few would help – especially since it might help you decide whether your Member of Parliament is a bloviating idiot or actually up to the job of representing your interests.

The European Union (EU)
The UK aside, the European Union countries are: Austria, Belgium, Bulgaria, Croatia, Cyprus, Czech Republic, Denmark, Estonia, Finland, France, Germany, Greece, Hungary, Ireland, Italy, Latvia, Lithuania, Luxembourg, Malta, Netherlands, Poland, Portugal, Romania, Slovakia, Slovenia, Spain, and Sweden.

European Economic Area (EEA)

The European Economic Area is the EU states plus Iceland, Liechtenstein and Norway. This allows Iceland, Liechtenstein and Norway to be part of the EU single market too. Confusingly, Switzerland is neither in the EU nor EEA but is also part of the single market, meaning Swiss nationals have the same rights to live and work in the UK as other EEA nationals.

European Free Trade Association (EFTA)

The European Free Trade Association (EFTA) is a trading club of four small nations: Iceland, Liechtenstein, Norway and Switzerland. It was set up in 1960 by seven member states (including the UK, which then left) for the promotion of free trade and economic integration between its members.

The Single Market

The Single European Act of 1992, enshrined the 'four freedoms' of movement in goods, services, capital and workers. While the first three have proved relatively uncontroversial within the UK, the free movement of workers (often, incorrectly, termed the free movement of people) became increasingly contentious after the accession of the countries of Central and Eastern Europe in 2004 and 2007. To date, UK government policy remains focused on bringing the free movement of workers to an end. By implication, this requires departure from the single market and therefore an end to the UK's membership of the wider European Economic Area (EEA, *see above*).

The Customs Union

Members of the EU customs union apply the same tariffs to imported goods from the rest of the world. Brussels negotiates trade deals on behalf of all EU members, and national governments then approve any final arrangement. The EU has trade deals covering 69 countries, including several negotiated in the past years such as with Canada, Japan, and Singapore. So far the UK has been unable to 'roll over' most of these deals to a post-Brexit Britain.

Ardent Brexiters, such as the Conservative's Liam Fox, say Britain must pursue an independent trade policy to best exploit the fast-growing economies of China, India and Brazil etc. In order to make its own arrangements with those countries, Britain must be able to set its own tariffs for the importation of goods, and so cannot be a member of the EU customs union.

Essentially, the choice facing Britain can be summed up as: rely on the dozens of trade deals negotiated by the big and experienced trade team in Brussels (and stay in the EU customs union) or strike out on its own as a smaller power and negotiate bespoke deals.

The World Trade Organisation (WTO)

The World Trade Organisation (WTO) is a global organisation which helps set the rules of trade between nations, who agree deals between themselves. The WTO has over 160 members representing 98 per cent of world trade. The European Union is a member of the WTO in its own right. Depending on the Brexit deal reached, that means that Britain might have to negotiate with all the other WTO members about the terms of its trade.

The Backstop

The Irish backstop is an insurance policy agreed by the UK and the EU to protect Ireland from the specific problems Brexit threatens to cause. Its aim is to avoid a 'hard border' (ie, a border with designated crossing points and manned checkpoints) between the Republic of Ireland and Northern Ireland. A hard border might be necessary because Northern Ireland is the only part of the UK which shares a land border with another country (and most importantly a country in the EU). To avoid that, the 'backstop' would come into force if no better solution to the problem is found. The backstop – which is hated by many Brexiters who dislike EU rules – would keep the UK tightly aligned to EU customs rules, while also allowing for some regulatory differences between Northern Ireland and the British mainland (making it also hated by Unionists who want Northern Ireland to be treated exactly the same as the rest of the United Kingdom).

Schengen Area

Austria, Belgium, Czech Republic, Denmark, Estonia, Finland, France, Germany, Greece Hungary, Iceland, Italy, Latvia, Liechtenstein, Lithuania, Luxembourg, Malta, the Netherlands, Norway, Poland, Portugal, Slovakia, Slovenia, Spain, Sweden and Switzerland.

ACKNOWLEDGEMENTS

This book was created thanks to the efforts of a great number of helpful people, but its biggest inspiration came from some unhelpful people. Among these were Nigel Farage and his Brexit Party plus their fellow travellers and enablers in the Conservative so-called 'European Research Group.' Day after day for the past three years these Brexiters have provided the British people with so many examples of factual mistakes, dodgy claims, errors, falsehoods, mis-statements, porkies, stretchers, whoppers, spin and downright lies, that correcting at least some of these fantasies became my principal motivation. I stand with those who believe that the normalisation of nonsense in British public life must be actively resisted. This book is part of that struggle. It is designed as factual ammunition for those who feel it is essential to offer a corrective politicians who lied to us about Brexit and proved so profoundly incompetent in trying to implement it. At the time of writing these politicians still cannot agree what Brexit actually is.

I'd like to thank my editor and publisher Martin Hickman at Canbury Press for his persistence and sound judgement. This book was his idea. I resisted agreeing to write it for weeks, until Martin finally persuaded me that we needed to base the future of our country on facts about Brexit rather than the fantasies we had been sold. I'd also like to thank my agent Andrew Gordon for his wisdom and advice, and the many people who have helped me positively or inspired me during the research. Among them are Ian Dunt, Alex Andreou, the Remaniacs Podcast, 16 Million Rising, the activists at SODEM, Steve Bray, Barbara Want, the People's Vote campaigners, Alastair Campbell, Tony Blair, Tom Baldwin, Carole Tongue, Alex Deane, Chuka Umunna, Chris Leslie, Heidi Allen, Dr Sarah Wollaston, Seb Dance, Charles Tannock, Mike Gapes, Jo Swinson, Bridget Phillipson, and many others including Twitter friends such as Dr Rachel Clarke, James Melville and countless others in various businesses and enterprises. I particularly enjoyed the conversations I had with London voters during the 2019 European Election campaign.

Any mistakes or omissions are mine. Above all I'd like to thank my wife, Anna, and my children, Charlotte, James, Amelia and Lucy. This book is dedicated to them. I hope it helps inspire us all towards a better future in which Brexit is no longer discussed, except as a historical curiosity.

Gavin Esler
London, June 2019

ENDNOTES

Introduction
1 Britain has had enough of experts, says Gove, *Financial Times*, 3 June 2016.
W https://www.ft.com/content/3be49734-29cb-11e6-83e4-abc22d5d108c

Chapter 1. Brexit & Our Food
2 What Europeans Talk about when They Talk about Brexit, *London Review of Books*, 3 January 2019**W** https://www.lrb.co.uk/v41/n01/on-brexit/what-europeans-talk-about-when-they-talk-about-brexit

3 May drops £65 fee for EU nationals seeking post-Brexit settled status, *The Guardian*, 21 January 2019. **W** https://www.theguardian.com/politics/2019/jan/21/may-drops-65-fee-for-eu-nationals-seeking-post-brexit-settled-status

4 Migrants in the UK Labour Market: An Overview, 31 July 2018, The Migration Observatory, University of Oxford. **W** https://migrationobservatory.ox.ac.uk/resources/briefings/migrants-in-the-uk-labour-market-an-overview/

5 Meat industry Workforce, British Meat Processors Association.**W** https://britishmeatindustry.org/industry/workforce/

6 The Impact of Brexit on the UK Soft fruit Industry, 3 December 2018, British Summer Fruits. **W** https://www.britishsummerfruits.co.uk/news

7 Migration Advisory Committee: Call for Evidence, Royal College of Veterinary Surgeons/British Veterinary Association. **W** https://www.rcvs.org.uk/document-library/joint-rcvs-and-bva-submission-to-migration-advisory-committee/

8 Migration Advisory Committee: Call for Evidence, Royal College of Veterinary Surgeons/British Veterinary Association. **W** https://www.bva.co.uk/uploadedFiles/Content/News,campaigns_and_policies/Get_involved/Consultation_archive/Migration%20Advisory%20Committee%20BVA%20RCVS%20Submission%20FINAL.PDF

9 Ibid.

10 Poll: How would you vote in a second EU referendum?, *Farmers Weekly*, 11 December 2018. **W** https://www.fwi.co.uk/news/eu-referendum/poll-how-would-you-vote-in-a-second-eu-referendum

11 EU Migration to and from the UK, The Migration Observatory, University of Oxford. **W** https://migrationobservatory.ox.ac.uk/resources/briefings/eu-migration-to-and-from-the-uk/

12 Britain's EU workforce in decline as numbers from elsewhere soar, *The Guardian*, 19 February 2019. **W** https://www.theguardian.com/uk-news/2019/feb/19/britain-eu-workforce-decline-numbers-elsewhere-soar-brexit

13 European fruit pickers shun Britain, *BBC News*, 7 June 2018. **W** https://www.bbc.co.uk/news/business-44230865

14 What will happen to the UK's European farm workers? BBC News, 4 July 2016.**W** https://www.bbc.co.uk/news/magazine-36656969

15 Lincolnshire records UK's highest Brexit vote , *BBC News*, 24 June 2016.**W** https://www.bbc.co.uk/news/uk-politics-eu-referendum-36616740

16 Origins of food consumed in the UK 2017, National Statistics. **W** https://www.gov.uk/government/publications/food-statistics-pocketbook-2017/food-statistics-in-your-pocket-2017-global-and-uk-supply#origins-of-food-consumed-in-the-uk-2017

17 Can the UK feed itself after Brexit?, 5 January 2018, *Countryfile Magazine*,
W https://www.countryfile.com/news/can-the-uk-feed-itself-after-brexit/

18 The Future of Food: Prof Tim Lang, Borough Market, 13 February 2017.
W http://boroughmarket.org.uk/articles/the-future-of-food-prof-tim-lang

19 Report reveals scale of food bank use in the UK, *The Guardian*, 29 May 2017.
W https://www.theguardian.com/society/2017/may/29/report-reveals-scale-of-food-bank-use-in-the-uk-ifan

20 Could Brexit mean increased prices in fruit imports from the EU? *Euronews.com*, 23 November 2017. **W** https://www.euronews.com/2017/11/23/which-of-your-favourite-fruit-imports-might-be-impacted-by-brexit

21 Could Brexit mean increased prices in fruit imports from the EU? Euronews.com, 23 November 2017. **W** https://www.euronews.com/2017/11/23/which-of-your-favourite-fruit-imports-might-be-impacted-by-brexit

22 Thefutureoffarmingpost-Brexit:aforeigncountry?TheCampaigntoProtectRuralEngland.**W**https://www.cpre.org.uk/magazine/opinion/item/4794-the-future-of-farming-post-brexit-a-foreign-country

23 Opinion of the Scientific Panel on food additives, flavourings, processing aids and materials in contact with food on a request from the Commission related to treatment of poultry carcasses with chlorine dioxide, acidified sodium chlorite, trisodium phosphate and peroxyacids, European Food Safety Authority. **W** http://www.efsa.europa.eu/sites/default/files/scientific_output/files/main_documents/297.pdf

24 Comment from National Grain and Feed Association & North American Export Grain Association on the Office of United States Trade Representative (USTR) Notice: Negotiating Objectives for a U.S.-United Kingdom Trade Agreement, Regulations.gov.**W** https://www.regulations.gov/document?D=USTR-2018-0036-0093

25 Evidence of Craig Thorn, Public Hearing on Negotiating Objectives for a US-UK Trade Agreement, 29 January 2019.**W**https://ustr.gov/sites/default/files/0129USTR.pdf

26 Review on Antimicrobial Resistance. **W** https://amr-review.org/sites/default/files/160525_Final%20paper_with%20cover.pdf

27 US firms seek changes to UK standards on beef and drugs, *BBC News*, 29 January 2019.**W** https://www.bbc.co.uk/news/business-47036119

28 I swallowed the Brexit lies. Now I regret telling curry house workers to vote leave, *The Guardian*, 15 February 2019. **W** https://www.theguardian.com/commentisfree/2019/feb/15/brexit-lies-curry-vote-leave-restaurant-industry

2. Brexit & the NHS

29 Letter from Sir David Norgrove, UK Statistics Authority, 17 September 2017.
W   https://www.statisticsauthority.gov.uk/wp-content/uploads/2017/09/Letter-from-Sir-David-Norgrove-to-Foreign-Secretary.pdf

30 Nigel Farage, Common Sense Tour, Public Meeting, Alfriston, 24 September 2012, YouTube.**W** https://www.youtube.com/watch?time_continue=2&v=dXBU68nTQj0

31 Brexit: most doctors and nurses now think NHS will get worse, *The Guardian*, 13 October 2018. **W** https://www.theguardian.com/politics/2018/oct/13/brexit-doctors-and-nurses-nhs-will-get-worse

32   Mirror, Mirror 2017: International Comparison Reflects Flaws and Opportunities for Better U.S. Health Care, The Commonwealth Fund, 2017. W https://interactives.commonwealthfund.org/2017/july/mirror-mirror/

33   UK economy since the Brexit vote: slower GDP growth, lower productivity, and a weaker pound, LSE. W https://blogs.lse.ac.uk/europpblog/2019/03/22/uk-economy-since-the-brexit-vote-slower-gdp-growth-lower-productivity-and-a-weaker-pound/

34   Fact checking Sir Michael Rawlins statements in relation to Insulin and #Brexit. Should we be worried?, Diabettech, 28 July 2018. W https://www.diabettech.com/brexit/fact-checking-sir-michael-rawlins-statements-in-relation-to-insulin-and-brexit-should-we-be-worried/

35   Over the edge: a no deal Brexit and the NHS, Nuffield Trust, 2 August 2018. W https://www.nuffieldtrust.org.uk/news-item/over-the-edge-a-no-deal-brexit-and-the-nhs

36   Homerton Hospital worker responds to EU Referendum result with photo of his NHS team, Hackney Gazette, 28 June 2016.W https://www.hackneygazette.co.uk/news/homerton-hospital-doctor-responds-to-eu-referendum-result-with-photo-of-his-nhs-team-1-4595398

37   Preparing for Brexit: social care, 23 November 2017, Nuffield Trust.W https://www.nuffieldtrust.org.uk/news-item/preparing-for-brexit-social-care

38   Getting a Brexit Deal that Works for the NHS, Nuffield Trust, 31 May 2017.W https://www.nuffieldtrust.org.uk/research/getting-a-brexit-deal-that-works-for-the-nhs

39   EHICcups on the Road to Brexit, Nuffield Trust, 17 January 2017. W https://www.nuffieldtrust.org.uk/news-item/ehiccups-on-the-road-to-brexit?

40   NHS could face bill of over half a billion pounds from Brexit, Nuffield Trust, 31 May 2017.Whttps://www.nuffieldtrust.org.uk/news-item/nhs-could-face-bill-of-over-half-a-billion-pounds-from-brexit

41   The NHS workforce in numbers, Nuffield Trust. W https://www.nuffieldtrust.org.uk/resource/the-nhs-workforce-in-numbers

42   Brexit will cause significant harm to the NHS, but No-Deal Brexit presents by far the worst option, London School of Hygiene & Tropical Medicine, 25 February 2019.W https://www.lshtm.ac.uk/newsevents/news/2019/brexit-will-cause-significant-harm-nhs-no-deal-brexit-presents-far-worst

43   The Ideal U.S.-U.K. Free Trade Agreement, Initiative for Free Trade, 2018. W http://ifreetrade.org/pdfs/US-UK-FTA.pdf

44   Jaguar Land Rover boss warns tens of thousands of jobs at risk if no Brexit deal reached, 11 September 2018.W https://www.independent.co.uk/news/business/news/jaguar-land-rover-jobs-risk-brexit-no-deal-ralf-speth-a8532876.html

3: Brexit, Our Jobs & Our Money

45   UK unemployment rate drops to lowest level since 1974, 14 May 2019. W https://www.ft.com/content/4cce6f54-7624-11e9-bbad-7c18c0ea0201

46   Contracts that do not guarantee a minimum number of hours: April 2018, Office of National Statistics.W https://www.ons.gov.uk/employmentandlabourmarket/peopleinwork/earningsandworkinghours/articles/contractsthatdonotguaranteeaminimumnumberofhours/april2018

47   The Fiscal Impact of Immigration on the UK, June 2018. W https://www.oxfordeconomics.com/recent-releases/8747673d-3b26-439b-9693-0e250df6dbba

48   'The analysis suggests that since the vote in June 2016, we have lost 2% of GDP relative to a scenar-

io where there had been no significant domestic economic events. That amounts to around 40 billion pounds per year, or 800 million per week of lost income for the country as a whole', The Economic Outlook: Fading global tailwinds, intensifying Brexit headwinds, speech by Gertjan Vlieghe, External Member of the Monetary Policy Committee, Bank of England, 14 February 2019. W https://www.bankofengland.co.uk/-/media/boe/files/speech/2019/the-economic-outlook-speech-by-gertjan-vlieghe.pdf.

49   The Brexit Vote, Inflation and UK Living Standards, LSE. W http://cep.lse.ac.uk/pubs/download/brexit11.pdf

50   Visit to the United Kingdom of Great Britain and Northern Ireland, Report of the Special Rapporteur on extreme poverty and human rights, United Nations, April 2019. W https://undocs.org/A/HRC/41/39/Add.1

51   Crispin Odey interview, *BBC News*. W https://www.youtube.com/watch?v=yCWaUnIBq90

52   Brexiteer Odey bets £500m AGAINST British businesses: Rees-Mogg backer hopes to gain from 'short' stakes in shares he believes will fall… , *Thisismoney.co.uk*, 9 June 2018. W https://www.thisismoney.co.uk/money/investing/article-5824697/Brexiteer-Odey-bets-500m-AGAINST-British-businesses.html

53   Brexit warning from investment firm co-founded by Rees-Mogg, *The Guardian*, 14 June 2018.   W   https://www.theguardian.com/politics/2018/jun/14/brexit-warning-investment-firm-somerset-capital-management-jacob-rees-mogg

54   Lord Ashcroft praises Malta as base for UK business during Brexit, *The Guardian*, 29 June 2018. W https://www.theguardian.com/politics/2018/jun/29/lord-ashcroft-praises-malta-as-base-for-uk-business-during-brexit

55   Dyson to move head office to Singapore, *BBC News*, 22 January 2019. W https://www.bbc.co.uk/news/business-46962093

56   What Can We Expect From Markets in 2019 – and just what will Brexit's Final Impact be?, 26 February 2019. W https://www.dynamicplanner.com/2019-market-expectations-brexit-impact/

57   Brexit could see $911 billion of assets siphoned from the City of London to Frankfurt, *Business Insider*, 29 November 2018. W https://www.businessinsider.com/brexit-london-will-lose-800-billion-of-assets-to-germany-2018-11?

58   Nearly a third of firms looking overseas due to Brexit, 1 February 2019, W https://www.iod.com/news/news/articles/Nearly-a-third-of-firms-looking-overseas-due-to-Brexit

59   Brexit will cut thousands of jobs and forfeit billions in tax, *Financial Times*, 11 December 2018. W https://www.ft.com/content/94d7d596-f961-11e8-af46-2022a0b02a6c

Brexit & Our Children's Education

60   The Economic Impact of Universities, 2017, Oxford Economics. W https://www.universitiesuk.ac.uk/policy-and-analysis/reports/Documents/2017/the-economic-impact-of-universities.pdf

61   England's schools face staffing crisis as EU teachers stay at home, The Observer, 12 January 2019 W https://www.theguardian.com/education/2019/jan/12/schools-staff-crisis-eu-teacher-applications-fall
62   'The impact of Brexit on education is immeasurable', *TES*, 27 September 2018. W https://www.tes.com/news/impact-brexit-education-immeasurable

63   Schools will be left 'exposed' by Brexit, 10 December 2018. W https://www.tes.com/news/schools-will-be-left-exposed-brexit

64   British schools explore EU expansion after Brexit, *Financial Times*, 4 January 2019. W https://www.ft.com/content/b777ee3a-06e8-11e9-9fe8-acdb36967cfc

65   Open letter - Leading school organisations call for Brexit negotiators to consider impact on schools and pupils, British Council, 30 April 2018. W https://www.britishcouncil.org/contact/press/open-letter-leading-school-organisations-call-brexit-negotiators-consider-impact-schools

66   Impact of International Students in the UK, Migration Advisory Committee. September 2018. W   https://assets.publishing.service.gov.uk/government/uploads/system/uploads/attachment_data/file/739089/Impact_intl_students_report_published_v1.1.pdf

67   England: fee status, 10 April 2019. W https://www.ukcisa.org.uk/Information--Advice/Fees-and-Money/England-fee-status

68   EU students get post-Brexit fees promise, *BBC News*, 2 July 2018. W https://www.bbc.co.uk/news/education-44676843

69   Fall in EU student numbers, Russell Group, 4 January 2019.W https://russellgroup.ac.uk/news/fall-in-eu-student-numbers/

5. Brexit & Travel

70   Stretched UK Border Force 'resourced to fail' and unable to stop illegal entry, *Daily Telegraph*, 13 November 2018. W https://www.telegraph.co.uk/news/2018/11/13/stretched-uk-border-force-resourced-fail-unable-stop-illegal/

71   Brexit: Will flights be disrupted?, *BBC News*, 31 March 2019. W https://www.bbc.co.uk/news/uk-47225806

72   Mobile firms refuse to rule out return of roaming charges after Brexit, *Moneysavingexpert.com*, 1 February 2019.   W   https://www.moneysavingexpert.com/news/2019/02/mobile-firms-not-ruling-out-roaming-charges-after-brexit/

73   Prepare to drive in the EU after Brexit, UK Government, 17 April 2019.W https://www.gov.uk/guidance/prepare-to-drive-in-the-eu-after-brexit

74   Pet travel to Europe after Brexit, UK Government, 10 April 2019. W https://www.gov.uk/guidance/pet-travel-to-europe-after-brexit

6. Brexit & Our Country

75   End of Mission Statement of the Special Rapporteur on Contemporary Forms of Racism, Racial Discrimination, Xenophobia and Related Intolerance at the Conclusion of Her Mission to the United Kingdom of Great Britain and Northern Ireland. W https://www.ohchr.org/en/NewsEvents/Pages/DisplayNews.aspx?NewsID=23073&LangID=E

76   Hate crime is up – but it's not fair to blame Brexit, *The Spectator*, 17 October 2017.W https://blogs.spectator.co.uk/2017/10/hate-crime-is-up-but-its-not-fair-to-blame-brexit/

77   Hate crime did spike after the referendum – even allowing for other factors, LSE W https://blogs.lse.ac.uk/brexit/2018/03/19/hate-crime-did-spike-after-the-referendum-even-allowing-for-other-factors/

78   The uncomfortable costs of moving Trident, *The Guardian*, 10 July 2013.W https://www.theguardian.com/uk-news/2013/jul/10/costs-moving-trident-analysis

7. A No Deal Brexit

79   Brexit: The impact on UK trade and living standards, Centre for Economic Performance, LSE, 2016. W http://cep.lse.ac.uk/pubs/download/cp469.pdf

Also by Canbury Press

Brexit: What the Hell Happens Now?
Ian Dunt
Paperback/Ebook/Audiobook